MW00440431

Finding the McCains

A Scots-Irish Odyssey

Barry R McCain

Ulster Heritage Publishing

PO Box 884
Oxford, Mississippi 38655
USA

© Barry R McCain 2015

All rights reserved. No part of this publication may be reproduced, stored in a retrieval system, or transmitted, in any form or by any means, without the prior permission in writing from Ulster Heritage Publishing, or as expressly permitted by law, or under terms agreed with the appropriate reprographics rights organizations. Enquiries concerning reproduction outside the scope of the above should be sent to Ulster Heritage Publishing at the address above.

ISBN 978-0-9855876-4-2

Acknowledgements

Many people helped me tremendously with my research for this book. Thanks goes out to Lou Poole in Texas, who is a first rate researcher, one of my McCain relations, and who sorted out the Colonial McCains. There are also the many McCains around the world, in Ireland, Scotland, the USA and Canada, who were absolutely crucial to this work, especially Jack MacKeen in Maynard, Massachusetts, and Jim McKane, in Wiarton, Ontario. A special thanks to Dr. William Roulston in County Antrim. Then I have a special thanks *agus go raibh maith agaibh* for help and hospitality to Austin and Mary Rock and family of Dublin and to Ivan and Letitia Knox and family, of Corcam, Donegal.

Preface

I am sitting at my desk in my home in the rolling wooded hills of north Mississippi, just outside Oxford and not far from the Ole Miss Campus. While sitting here I think on the 40 year journey I have been on, an odyssey to find the McCains that remained in Ireland. *Finding the McCains* is the story of one Mississippi McCain who made up his mind to find his cousins in Ireland and discover their history. This was not easy as we left Ireland circa 1718 and the trail was faint, but I succeeded. The themes of migration, Diaspora, genetic genealogy, re-joined family and clan, run through the book. It is a detective story, a memoir, a history, and a how-to guide for genetic genealogy. In a perfect world I would have had this book ready in early 2008 when my cousin, Senator John McCain, was making his bid for the White House. We were a popular brand that year, but the story kept growing in scope. The research made breakthroughs in 2009 through 2014 that allowed a more complete history to be written.

My motivation in researching the McCain family was simple, my love of family and tribe. It is called heritage and it gives me my place in the universe. The naming of one's ancestors is a profound act and it gives clarity and meaning to one's life. That is why people spend hours upon hours getting family history straight and writing it down for future generations to read and remember. This book is my tribute to my ancestors. Several times while I was researching and writing this story, I had the sensation that my grandparents were near to me even though they passed away many years ago. One day while I sat at my desk, old photographs and papers of genealogies scattered about, I seemed to catch the pleasant aroma that I associated with my Grandmother McCain. She was born in 1883 and used a lavender floral scent that was popular a century ago. It is difficult to explain such events. The world is more mysterious than we can imagine and perhaps at times our ancestors do visit us in some form or fashion. It is an interesting concept and one I find pleasing.

There are some elements of this story that could offend some readers. The South and Ulster both are capable of producing passionate feelings and rhetoric and it is also true that there is no quicker way to stir up trouble than to write about one's extended family. However, most of our extended family were very pleased with how the story turned out. I am the *seanchaí* and this is my account of finding the McCains.

Barry R McCain

December 2014

Note to Reader

In this book there are a variety of spellings of the McCain surname including McAne, Mac Eáin, McCain, McCane, McKaine, McKane, McKean, McKeen, and M'Ean, which are all read as "McCain." Each branch of the family has used many spellings of the name over the years. They are all anglicized spellings of the Gaelic surname, *Mac Eáin*. There are several McCain families from Ireland and Scotland. This book is about one particular McCain family that originated in Kilmichael Glassary parish in mid Argyll, Scotland.

The Gaelic spellings in the text are in modern Irish Gaelic orthography with some Ulster and Argyll dialect influences. Gaelic is used as a general label for the Goidelic language of Ireland and Scotland. "Irish" is used interchangeably with "Gaelic" when referencing language. Gaelic forms of personal names are used in many cases when referring to people prior to 1600 because of the complete inconsistency of anglicized forms. Geographic names follow the orthography of modern Ordnance Survey maps in most cases with some exceptions where I used a Gaelic spelling. The McCains are a Gaelic family and it would be impossible to tell their story without some use of the language.

Table of Contents

The Lagan

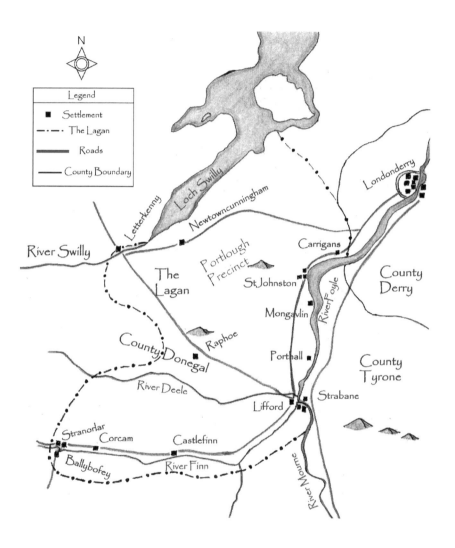

Teoc and Hill Country McCains direct line of descent only of families mentioned in the book

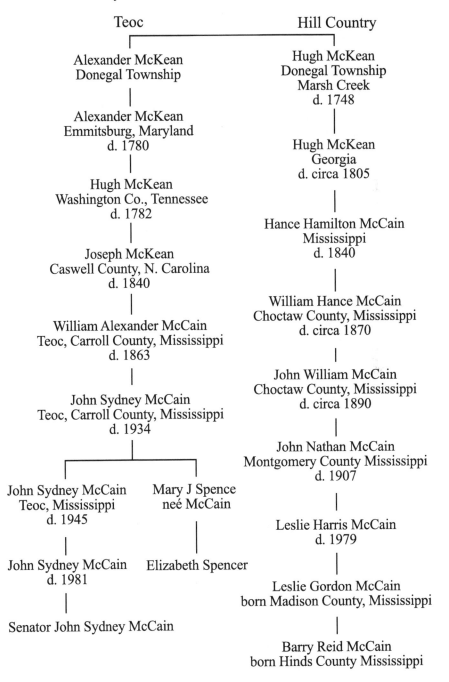

Teoc

Alexander McKean
Donegal Township

Alexander McKean
Emmitsburg, Maryland
d. 1780

Hugh McKean
Washington Co., Tennessee
d. 1782

Joseph McKean
Caswell County, N. Carolina
d. 1840

William Alexander McCain
Teoc, Carroll County, Mississippi
d. 1863

John Sydney McCain
Teoc, Carroll County, Mississippi
d. 1934

John Sydney McCain
Teoc, Mississippi
d. 1945

Mary J Spence
neé McCain

John Sydney McCain
d. 1981

Elizabeth Spencer

Senator John Sydney McCain

Hill Country

Hugh McKean
Donegal Township
Marsh Creek
d. 1748

Hugh McKean
Georgia
d. circa 1805

Hance Hamilton McCain
Mississippi
d. 1840

William Hance McCain
Choctaw County, Mississippi
d. circa 1870

John William McCain
Choctaw County, Mississippi
d. circa 1890

John Nathan McCain
Montgomery County Mississippi
d. 1907

Leslie Harris McCain
d. 1979

Leslie Gordon McCain
born Madison County, Mississippi

Barry Reid McCain
born Hinds County Mississippi

Partial Genealogies and land transfers in Glassary of Giolla Chríost and his descendants

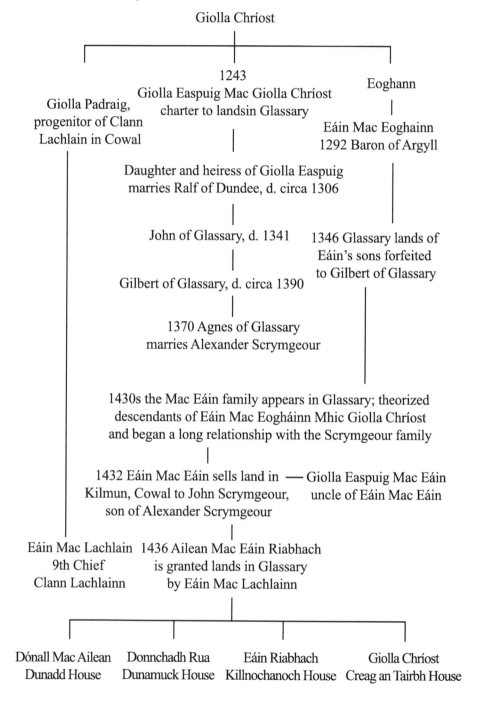

Giolla Chríost

1243
Giolla Easpuig Mac Giolla Chríost
charter to landsin Glassary

Giolla Padraig, progenitor of Clann Lachlain in Cowal

Eoghann

Eáin Mac Eoghainn
1292 Baron of Argyll

Daughter and heiress of Giolla Easpuig marries Ralf of Dundee, d. circa 1306

John of Glassary, d. 1341

1346 Glassary lands of Eáin's sons forfeited to Gilbert of Glassary

Gilbert of Glassary, d. circa 1390

1370 Agnes of Glassary marries Alexander Scrymgeour

1430s the Mac Eáin family appears in Glassary; theorized descendants of Eáin Mac Eogháinn Mhic Giolla Chríost and began a long relationship with the Scrymgeour family

1432 Eáin Mac Eáin sells land in — Giolla Easpuig Mac Eáin
Kilmun, Cowal to John Scrymgeour, uncle of Eáin Mac Eáin
son of Alexander Scrymgeour

Eáin Mac Lachlain
9th Chief
Clann Lachlainn

1436 Ailean Mac Eáin Riabhach is granted lands in Glassary by Eáin Mac Lachlainn

Dónall Mac Ailean
Dunadd House

Donnchadh Rua
Dunamuck House

Eáin Riabhach
Killnochanoch House

Giolla Chríost
Creag an Tairbh House

Introduction

As a child I was a reader of history books and the lore of the past thrilled me. I read of David Crockett and his buckskin exploits, of Cortez and his amazing conquests, of Vikings and Crusaders. It was all wonderful to a young towheaded Southern boy. One day I was reading a history of the Elizabethan English and their wars of conquest against the Irish in Ulster. I noticed that many of the Irish and their Scottish allies had names beginning with Mac or O. I read a passage which quoted Elizabethan writer Edmund Spencer who was lamenting the "Oes and the Mackes" and wanting the use of Gaelic surname prefixes to be "utterly forbidden and extinguished." I put the book down struck by the thought, *hey, I am one of those Mac fellows*. I was around 12 years old at the time. I poured over the encyclopedias at our local library for hours researching the subject and a new world opened up to me. My surname was Gaelic and I was one of these Gaels, though now far removed from my origins. My people were the ones causing the English all that trouble so many years ago. Not only that, but we had our own language and culture. I was delighted.

That was the beginning of my long exploration to seek out and find my family in the land of the Macs and Os and to learn our history. My story begins with the McCain families in Mississippi, but, as often happens with stories, the tale grew and took on a life of its own. I discovered the Mississippi McCains were but a small part of a larger McCain family found in New Brunswick, Canada, in New England, and in Donegal, Ireland, and a half dozen other places. Like so many families of Ireland we migrated to many places around the world. What joins us together and gives us a shared history is we all have the same paternal ancestry. We all descend from one McCain man who lived in late medieval times, in mid Argyll, in the heart of the Scottish Highlands. The McCains migrated from Argyll to County Donegal, Ireland, in the 1500s. We began migrating to the New World in the eighteenth century as so many northern Irish families did. The McCains migrated in waves beginning in 1718, then another wave in the 1730s, and in 1750s, and the 1790s; all going to the English colonies and later to the young republic. Then the pattern changed. In the 1830s and 1840s, we migrated to Canada, to New Brunswick and to Ontario.

The McCain history includes people and events familiar to readers of Irish and Scottish history. Redshanks, Iníon Dubh, Mary Queen of Scots, the Earls of Argyll, the Ulster Migration, and the Scots-Irish are all part of this family's history. Faint memories of this past were told for generations here in Mississippi and as the research progressed the facts behind these memories were uncovered. The chapters dealing with McCain history are based upon primary source documents and Y chromosome DNA testing. The successful McCain family DNA project was absolutely crucial in locating the McCains in

Ireland and learning about our past. While this book includes a history of the McCains, it is more than a historical account. It is also a memoir of my experiences on my journey to find the McCains and a commentary on the relationship between Diaspora and Homeland.

This book will shed light on the Ulster Scots and their New World descendants the Scots-Irish. The Ulster Scots have a more complex story than is normally presented in most histories of them. By telling the story of the McCain family some of this complexity will be addressed. The McCains were Highland Scots and not Lowland Planters in Ulster and yet they became part of the Ulster Scot community in the 1600s. The reason for this is found in the history of the Highland Scots that migrated to Donegal in the 1500s.

The movement of Highland Scots, or Redshanks as they were called at that time, is an understudied aspect of Irish history. The migration of Redshanks to east Donegal was orchestrated by the powerful Clan Campbell of Argyll. The head of this clan in the mid-1500s was the fifth Earl of Argyll, Giolla Easpuig Donn Caimbeul. He led a successful military campaign in Donegal for the O'Donnell clan early in his career and later became involved in political and military matters in Ulster. The fifth Earl of Argyll was the catalyst that led not only the McCains, but many other Highland Scots, to settle along the banks of the Foyle River in east Donegal and northwest Tyrone. These Redshanks lived through the Elizabethan attempts to subdue Ulster in the late 1500s and remained on their lands as the Plantation of Ulster began in 1609. It was a time of great cultural change, but the Redshanks found a place within the New Order established by the

Plantation of Ulster. They became Irish, albeit with a footnote to them.

When the Ulster Migration to the Colonies began in 1718 the McCains were literally on the first organized fleet and were co-leaders of the expedition. They became quintessential Scots-Irish and many of them followed the frontier west and south. Several branches of the McCains settled in Mississippi.

The Mississippi McCains

I am one of the Mississippi McCains. We descend from archetypical Ulster settlers that arrived in the Colonies in the early 1700s. We are what popular history likes to call Scots-Irish. This, on the face of it, seems fairly straight forward, but I discovered that it is a complex ethnic designation full of little known history and anecdotes.

Scots-Irish is an old term dating to the mid-1500s and its meaning has changed over the centuries since it first came into use. In the 1500s to the late 1600s, Scots-Irish referred specifically to Highland and Hebridean Gaels living in Ulster. The term began to change in meaning in Colonial America and it began to be used to describe Protestant Irish settlers. Most of these Protestant Irish settlers were of Lowland Scots ancestry, though not all were.

By the late 1800s, the term Scots-Irish was used to draw a distinction between the newer immigrants from the older immigrants who were already established in America. In general, it is accurate to say that the first migration was mainly from Ulster. The second migration, which began in the 1840's, was from the whole of Ireland. The separation of these Irish immigrants into two groups has a lot to do with ethnic myth building. Canadian historian, Donald Akenson, has demonstrated that the historical paradigm of the second migration being largely urban and northern is not true.[1] Perhaps, the main differences between the two groups was that the first migration was largely Protestant and arrived when there was still a frontier to be conquered, whereas the second migration was largely Catholic and arrived after the United States was a nation.

To understand the McCains it is necessary to have a basic understanding of the Scots-Irish and their history. The McCains fit both the older original definition of Scots-Irish and the newer one that came into use in New World. This fact is important in the telling of not only the McCain history, but also in understanding an important aspect of Scots-Irish history as well.

The Mississippi McCains are well known in our humble state. Various branches of them have *done well*. Our ranks include a university president, generals, admirals, musicians, physicians, and farmers.[2] The McCain homelands in Mississippi are located in the north central part of the state, in Carroll, Montgomery, Choctaw, and Webster counties. There are also branches of them in Grenada and Lafayette counties and they have moved to many other places in the state over time. As you drive south from Memphis on I-55 near Grenada,

---

[1] Donald Harman Akenson, *Being Had: Historians, Evidence, and the Irish in North America.* (Ontario: P.D. Meany Company, 1985), sic passim.
[2] A short list of McCain luminaries with Mississippi roots: Admiral John Sidney McCain Sr., Admiral John Sidney McCain Jr., Major General Henry Pinckney McCain, Brigadier General William A McCain, Dr. William D McCain, president of University of Southern Mississippi, Elizabeth Spencer.

Mississippi, you will pass a large sign proclaiming the location of Camp McCain. It is a military training camp that has been in operation since WW II and is named after Major General Henry P. McCain who served in the Philippines during the Spanish American War. He was from a tiny place called Teoc, Mississippi, which brings us to where we need to be in this story. The light of the Teoc McCains shines bright indeed.

Two of the more prominent contemporary Teoc McCains are Senator John McCain and author Elizabeth Spencer. Teoc in Carroll County, Mississippi, is a little community that grew up around the plantation of William Alexander McCain. William Alexander McCain named his plantation Waverly, but the original Choctaw name of the area stuck and the area is called Teoc to this day. The Choctaw word *Teoc* is a shortened form of *Teoc Tillila* which means Tall Pines. William Alexander McCain is the great great grandfather of Senator John McCain.

Teoc is an unincorporated community and is known not only for its association with the McCains, but is also famous as the birthplace of music legend Mississippi John Hurt. John Hurt's mother was Mary Jane McCain, a black woman who was from the McCain Plantation at Teoc. If she had her name from the McCain plantation or if there is a bloodline connection, I do not know, as that was outside my field of study. John Hurt's granddaughter is Mary Hurt-Wright, who runs the Mississippi John Hurt Museum in Carrollton. John Hurt played a mellow, melodic, finger picking style of guitar which incorporated country, blues, and old time music. It is some of the best music ever to come out of Mississippi, which is saying a lot as this state has produced a wealth of famous musicians from Elvis Presley and B. B. King, to Marty Stuart.

There are still McCains in and around Teoc. Bill McCain, a descendant of patriarch William Alexander McCain, still owns land in the area that was part of the original plantation. In the small town of Carrollton, near Teoc, there is the Merrill Museum, which houses the John Sidney McCain Collection, a compilation of personal and military memorabilia belonging to several prominent McCains including Admiral John Sidney McCain Sr., grandfather of Senator John McCain. John Sidney McCain Sr. attended Ole Miss and then went to the Naval Academy. In time he was promoted to admiral and became known as Admiral "Slew" McCain, a pivotal and important naval commander in the Pacific during WW II. Senator McCain's father, John Sidney McCain II, served as a naval officer in WW II. For much of the war he was a submarine commander and saw combat in the Pacific theater, sinking several Japanese ships. Like his father, he also rose to the rank of admiral during the Vietnam War.

John McCain's own career and accomplishments are well known. He is a former naval aviator with a distinguished service record. He flew many combat missions over North Vietnam. While on a bombing mission over Hanoi in October 1967, McCain was shot down, seriously wounded and captured. Repeatedly tortured in captivity, he refused politically motivated offers of early release by the North Vietnamese. He remained a prisoner of war until his release in 1973. He retired from the Navy in 1981 and moved to Arizona where he entered politics. He served first in the US House of Representatives and was then elected as senator from Arizona in 1986. He has a McCainian reputation as a *maverick* and has a talent and willingness to disagree with people, even in his own party, on certain issues. John McCain unsuccessfully ran for the Republican presidential nomination in 2000 against George W. Bush. He won the nomination in 2008, but lost to the Democratic candidate, Barack Obama in the general election. The less said about that unfortunate matter the better.

Author Elizabeth Spencer is a first cousin once removed to John McCain. That is to say she is the daughter of Senator McCain's paternal grandfather's sister. Elizabeth Spencer is a talented and accomplished writer of novels and short stories. She could walk into a room with William Faulkner and Eudora Welty and take her place among them. As Eudora Welty herself put it:

> It has never been doubted that Elizabeth Spencer knows the small, Southern, backwoods hilltown down to the bone. This she transforms by the accuracy of her eye and ear, talent and a certain prankish gaiety of spirit into a vital and absorbing novel.[3]

Perhaps the best known work of Elizabeth Spencer would be her 1960 short novel *The Light of the Piazza*. It is a poignant story set in Italy that was made into a feature film in 1962 staring Olivia de Havilland, George Hamilton, and Yvette Mimieux. Elizabeth is still writing at age 93, her latest work is *Starting Over,* a collection of short stories. I enjoyed her

[3] Elizabeth Spencer, *Writer's website,*
http://www.elizabethspencerwriter.com.

company recently in Oxford, Mississippi and our talk turned naturally to the McCains and their history.

I mention Senator McCain and Elizabeth Spencer as they both have autobiographies with short accounts of the McCain history in them. Senator McCain published *Faith of Our Fathers* in 1999 and Elizabeth Spencer published her memoir, *Landscapes of The Heart* in 1998. In both books there is McCain lore and something of an origin story. The story goes like this; the McCains were a Scottish Highland family that somehow became involved in the politics and conflict that surrounded Mary Queen of Scots and at some time after her downfall had to flee the Highlands for Ireland, presumably in the late 1560s. Senator McCain's version incorporates connections to the famous Scottish Clan Donald. Both stories mention the Presbyterian faith of the McCains, which is interesting given the fact that they were supporting the Catholic Queen Mary.

I found Elizabeth Spencer's description of her McCains interesting as I recognized the characteristic of the clan in her observation. She has a chapter in *Landscapes of the Heart* titled *The McCains* in which she writes:

> The whole McCain connection bore an aura of an outside world. They were related permanently to Teoc and Carrollton, but they knew and were known, recognized, skilled, and active in the bigger world beyond.[4]

---

[4] Elizabeth Spencer, *Landscapes of the Heart* (New York: Random House, 1998), 13.

I think that is a fair assessment of the McCain clan and something I have observed in most of them, including the branches of them still in Ireland and our Diaspora. We tend to be very connected to home, hearth, and the land, yet also think outside of our region and we seem to be possessed with seeking accomplishments there.

Teoc is prime plantation country on the edge of the Mississippi Delta. My own branch of the McCains lived to the east of Teoc. As you travel east from Teoc, you leave the rich farm lands of the Mississippi Delta and head into the Mississippi Hill Country. Its hills are a place of small farms rather than large plantations. My great grandfather and grandfather were born in the Hill County and were small holding farmers. My generation was the first in my branch to make it to the hallowed halls of Ole Miss. The Teoc branch beat us there by some 70 years, which I think reflects the difference between a plantation and a hill country farm. Senator John McCain is my father's eighth cousin. My Hill Country McCains share immigrant ancestors with the Teoc branch. The Teoc group and my Hill Country group descend from McCain cousins that moved into Mississippi in the 1830s when Andrew Jackson opened up the Choctaw Indian lands for settlement.

My grandfather was born in Vaiden, in Carroll County, Mississippi, which is about 30 miles southeast of Teoc. I did not find out the exact relationship of the branches of these Mississippi McCains until I had completed many years of research. Growing up, I was informed that we were all indeed kin. But kinship is a vague concept to a child. Like many people that become interested in family history, I later regretted not asking more questions. Now, after many years of research and DNA testing, I could list pages and pages of McCains and in-laws showing the degrees of familial connections. But this is not a genealogy. It is the story of how I found the McCains in the old country and learned their real history.

Where to start the tale? I will mention a few ancestors to show how this Ulster Irish family spread and how the Mississippi branch came into being. This is only fitting as it was a Mississippi McCain that made the long journey back to Ireland and found our people that remained there. From Mississippi to Ireland is a great stretch in geography and in time. It was a long journey for me, one I became obsessed with. I made many trips to Ireland and Scotland. I learned Gaelic, received a history degree from Ole Miss, and met many interesting people along the path. Some were controversial by today's thin skinned standards, but I include them as they are part of the tale. This story could start in Ireland or Scotland, but there is an important point in the history of both Ireland and the McCains that determined for me where we should start. That point is the year 1718. In that year the first organized migration of Presbyterians left the north of Ireland for a new way of life in the English Colonies in North America.

1718

The McCains are an Ulster family. Ulster conjures up many images and thoughts to even those who are not of Ireland. Ulster is the northern province of Ireland and is comprised of nine counties, Antrim, Armagh, Down, Fermanagh, Derry, and Tyrone in Northern Ireland, and Cavan, Donegal, and Monaghan in the Republic of Ireland. That is the geography of it, but Ulster is so much more. Ulster for a long time has been a place of conflict and war and has its share of tragic history. Yet Ulster is also a place of sublime natural beauty, of mountains, glens, forests and seashore. It is a land of Celtic magic and lore and of wonderful people with rich traditions. It has traditional music, excellent food and drink, and a quality of life that is rare. In Ulster's long history, one of the most important events took place in 1718 and the McCains were an integral part of it.

In the late summer of 1718, six ships arrived in Boston harbor from Ireland. These ships and the families aboard them were the first organized migration of Irish-born Presbyterians to the New England colonies in North America. The event is called the 1718 Migration and it is remembered and celebrated in Ulster to this day. The ships were:

The William and Mary from Coleraine,
30 tons, with passengers and provisions.
The McCallum from Londonderry,
70 tons, 100 passengers and some linen.
The Mary and Elizabeth from Londonderry,
45 tons, some linen and 45 passengers.
The William and Elizabeth from Londonderry,
40 tons, passengers and provisions.
The Robert from Coleraine.
The William from Coleraine[5]

The Robert and *The William*, both out of Coleraine, arrived on 4 August carrying immigrants that were for the most part from the Bann Valley area. The Bann River runs north from Loch Neagh to the Irish Sea and this fertile valley lies in the counties of Antrim and Derry in what is now Northern Ireland. Ballymoney, Bushmills, and Coleraine are the main towns of the area. *The McCallum, The William and Mary, The Mary and Elizabeth, and the William and Elizabeth* arrived on 6 September. These ships also carried more Presbyterian families from east Donegal, Derry, northwest Tyrone, and more settlers from the Bann Valley.

While there had already been people from Ulster that had settled in the New World, the arrival of these ships is considered the *beginning* of a large migration of people from Ulster to the Colonies. The fleet brought a new migration paradigm of communities and groups of families migrating

---

[5] Dr James McConnell, Institute for Scots-Irish Studies, *The 1718 Migration*, http://www.1718migration.org.uk/s_home.asp. This website was created by the Ulster-Scots Agency in association with the Ulster Historical Foundation and the Centre for Migration Studies and the Institute of Ulster-Scots Studies.

18

together in a fleet of ships and settling as a community. This fleet was followed by many more from Ulster. In many ways, the 1718 fleet changed the history of North America as it introduced the seed from which would grow a race of frontiersmen and their families who created the United States. They were the people that pushed the frontier south and west. They made the trails and fought the Indians, the French, the British (and several other groups), allowing the Colonies and later the Republic to follow them.

They left Ireland to escape economic hardships and to pursue religious freedom. British restrictive trade legislation had severely impacted the Ulster economy prior to 1718. The downturn in the economy was coupled with the growing practice of *rack renting*. The tradition in land renting in Ireland was to lease a holding for around 30 years with an option to renew the rent at the same rate at the end of that time. This way the renter would be inclined to improve the property knowing that he would be able to pass his rented piece of land on to his heirs. This was the Irish land renting tradition and it provided security and a future for farming families. Rack renting broke with this tradition. The land owner would raise the rental rate and demand payment in cash. Money was extremely hard to come by in the early 1700s and families were pushed off of their land. Rack-renting and the economic downturn caused discontent to spread widely across Ulster and many families made the decision to leave Ireland for the Colonies.

There were additional factors that led to a growing desire for those who could, to migrate. Northern Ireland experienced drought from 1714 to 1719 which encouraged migration, but there were political catalysts as well. The repressive Penal Laws in the early 1700s were applied to Catholics and Presbyterians alike. All these factors led to the perfect storm for emigration. Most historians put the Ulster Migration as running from 1718 to circa 1775 and estimate some 250,000 Ulster folk left Ireland for the Colonies. These Ulster families tended to be large, seven to ten children per family was not unusual, so that 250,000 figure quickly grew to several million and they had a great impact upon the Colonies and early Republic.

There was a substantial McCain presence aboard this 1718 fleet including James McKeen and his family. James was a co-leader of the expedition and his family made the journey with him. There was also the widow and family of John McKeen, brother to James McKeen. John had helped plan and organize the expedition but passed away before the departure date. Another leader of the party was Rev. James McGregor, a popular and prominent Gaelic speaking Presbyterian minister and an in-law of the McKeens. Rev. McGregor had been active in the Bann Valley for many years. He was married to Mary Cargill, the sister of James McKeen's wife. Part of McGregor's duties as a minister was to preach and proselytize in Gaelic to the native Irish and Redshank communities in Antrim and Derry. To remind the reader, Redshanks were Highland Scottish Gaels that lived in Ireland and most of them were still Gaelic speaking in the early 1700s. McGregor was an interesting man; tall, powerfully built, and known for being a lover of ale. Most accounts of his life mention he participated in the defense of Derry during the siege of 1689. Participation in the Siege of Derry is an important aspect of Presbyterian Ulster Scot lore. It should be noted that Rev.

James McGregor was born in 1677 in County Londonderry and he was 12 years old during the siege. We shall say he was a stout young man and give him the benefit of the doubt.

Rev. McGregor preached in Ulster Irish. Ulster Irish is the Gaelic spoken in the north of Ireland and it shares some similarities to Scots Gaelic. Among the families on the six ships, both Gaelic and Lallans[6] were spoken and this made the Ulster folk linguistically and culturally alien from the already established Puritan community in New England. The Ulster settlers were not warmly received. There were complaints that the they were "poor Irish" and "not wholesome inhabitants" and even "Roman Catholics."[7] Rev. McGregor had to write to Massachusetts Governor, Samuel Shute, to assure him that they were in fact Presbyterians and were truly British subjects. Rev. James McGregor was a friend and in-law to the McCains and he also illustrates various elements that went into the making of the Scots-Irish community in the American Colonies. McGregor is a Highland Scottish surname from the Loch Lomond area. The communities of Highland Scots in Ulster participated in the eighteenth-century migration in large numbers, a fact rarely mentioned in most Scots-Irish histories.

James McKeen and Rev. McGregor were the co-leaders of a group of seventeen Presbyterian families from the Bann

---

[6] Lallans originated from northern English dialects and was spoken throughout much of the eastern Scottish Lowlands by the 1500s. It has influences from Latin and French due to the Auld Alliance as well as Dutch and Low German from trade with the Low Countries. It also has many Gaelic loan words. Lallans is often called Ullans in Ulster and the language is still spoken there today.
[7] Kerby A Miller, ed. and others, *Irish Immigrants In The Land of Canaan,* (Oxford: Oxford University Press, 2003), 438.

Valley that were aboard the *Robert* which sailed into Boston harbor on 4 August 1718. The McKeens and their relations were not poor despite the Puritan allegations. They were generally prosperous and travelled with letters of introduction to the local Colonial officials. These were men of some means on a great adventure and motivated by love of God and desire to live in a land away from the worsening economic and political problems in Ireland.

James McKeen was born in 1665, possibly in County Antrim, but it is hard to say for sure and he or his father may have been born in east County Donegal as it was there the McCains first settled in Ireland. He did have business interests and is associated with Ballymoney in County Antrim. His descendants in New England have an oral history of him owning interest in a ship building firm on the Foyle River near Derry city. There are still several McCain families that live on the Foyle at Port Hall, County Donegal.

James McKeen was a Presbyterian and active in that community. He had distinguished himself in the 1689 defense of Londonderry. In 1718, James McKeen was 53 years old and in the prime of life for a man of his grit. He had already had a very full life. He was a successful man of business and a leader within his community. He married Janet Cochran and had twelve children with her before she died in 1712. However, his greatest accomplishment still lay in front of him. James married the young Annis Cargill in 1713 and began a new family. He also began preparations to lead a group of families to the Colonies, which became the epic 1718 fleet.

Once in the New World, James McKeen continued his role as leader. After a cold and miserable winter of 1718/19, he led a group of three hundred or so Irish Presbyterians into the Merrimack Valley and founded the first European settlement there. This was in New Hampshire at Nutfield, so named for its abundance of hickory and walnut trees. The settlement was a success and in June of 1722 the charter for Londonderry, as they renamed Nutfield, was issued. James McKeen was the first magistrate commissioned in the town.

Reading accounts of these McKeen families was enlightening. The frontier was violent and death by Indian was common. Through all these hardships, however, the McKeens thrived. The descendants of James McKeen live in New England today and usually use the McKeen spelling of our surname. The graves of James McKeen and his family are located in the Forest Hill Cemetery in East Derry, New Hampshire. The families of John and James McKeen established branches throughout the northern Colonies. Some of these McKeens went to Truro, Nova Scotia, others stayed in New England and some of them migrated south to the Pennsylvania Colony.

The Mississippi McCains and the New England McKeens are the same family. I discovered this via DNA testing in 2003 when the McCain Family DNA project began. Not only are they the same family, but the DNA results placed the shared paternal ancestor as living in the mid-1600s, so the connection was very close in 1718. It was a bit of a shock to both parties to discover our close kinship as the New England McKeens are quintessential *Yankees* and the Mississippi McCains are quintessential *Confederates*. However, in 1718, we were all Ulstermen of the same family and closely related. The discovery of that kinship made the 1718 fleet and the New England McKeens part of my quest to find my family in Ireland. It also gave me a much better understanding of when the Mississippi McCains left Ireland and how they came to settle in Mississippi.

Donegal Township

The New England McKeens and Mississippi McCains have the same paternal line that leads back to a common paternal ancestor living in Ireland in the 1600s. DNA tests can confirm paternal kinship, but even with this wonderful research tool it is still sometimes difficult to make the entire story emerge from the fog of the past. One problem is that it is not always possible to discern between first cousins and brothers because they are genetically so close. But even given that, the DNA results did allow me to assemble a good history of the immigrant generation of the McCains that came into early Colonial America and made their way to Mississippi.

The McCains that settled in Mississippi make their first appearance in the Colonial tax records for Donegal settlement, Pennsylvania Colony, in 1722. The Donegal settlement was formally organized into a township in 1723 in a part of Conestoga County that is now in Lancaster County, Pennsylvania. Governments being what they are these McCains were taxed. Alexander McKean appears on the Donegal Township tax rolls in 1722 and he and his brother, Hugh McKean, appear on the list in 1724 through 1726 with a widow McKean listed for 1727. All the Mississippi McCains who have participated in DNA testing are descendants of Alexander and Hugh McKean.

Whether or not Alexander and Hugh McKean were on the 1718 fleet that came into Boston harbor cannot be said with absolute certainty. However, they were settled in the PA Colony by 1721 in order to be on the 1722 tax roll. Alexander and Hugh McKean either arrived with the 1718 fleet or followed their kinsmen sometime in the next two years. The history of the Londonderry, New Hampshire settlement suggests one explanation of how the Mississippi McCains came into the Pennsylvania Colony at that early date. The Londonderry settlement served as a staging area for Scots-Irish who established other settlements in the Colonies. It is possible that the progenitors of the Mississippi McCains were in Londonderry, New Hampshire, and moved to Donegal Township in 1721, or they could have come by another ship in 1719 or 1720.

There is an interesting story of Mary Wilson, known as Ocean Born Mary, who was born at sea aboard *The Wolf*. This ship sailed out of Coleraine with a group of Ulster Scot families bound for Boston in 1720. *The Wolf* was making the same run as James McKeen's fleet had done two years before. However, *The Wolf* was captured by pirates under Captain Pedro. The pirate captain heard the cries of the baby Mary, who had been born during the voyage, and was so touched that he allowed the Ulster Scots to resume their journey. They landed at Boston harbor and Mary and her mother made their way to the Londonderry, New Hampshire settlement established by James McKeen. While this all sounds pretty extraordinary, there is a McCain letter written in 1925 that mentions that our Mississippi McCains spent a short time in Bermuda before arriving in the Colonies. The letter was written by the granddaughter of a McCain born in the late 1790s. Whether or not this odd piece of McCain correspondence refers to a half remembered pirate intrigue or if the family tried their hand at some commercial venture in the islands is not known, but it is a curious bit of lore that suggests the story is based on fact.

There are many male descendants of the immigrants Alexander and Hugh McKean that have participated in the McCain DNA Project and they all are a paternal DNA match to each other and match the New England McKeens that led the 1718 fleet. The sons and grandsons of Alexander and Hugh McKean are the progenitors of many McCain branches from Pennsylvania south into the Carolinas, Georgia, Alabama, Tennessee, Mississippi, Texas and beyond. I will not present a genealogy of these many branches, but I will briefly outline two lines that settled in Mississippi and established the Teoc branch of Senator McCain and the Mississippi Hill Country branch of my line. This outline will illustrate how this Ulster family came to be in Mississippi.[8]

Alexander McKean stayed in the Donegal Township in what is now Lancaster County, Pennsylvania, but several of his sons, including one named Alexander McKean II, moved to the southern part of the Marsh Creek Settlement, which is today in Frederick County, Maryland. Hugh McKean of the Donegal Township also moved to the Marsh Creek Settlement, but north of the Maryland border into what is now Gettysburg, Pennsylvania.

---

[8] See Teoc and Hill Country McCains geneology on page 3.

The Marsh Creek settlement looms large in the history of Ulster and her people in the New World. From the 1730s through the 1760s it was the epicenter of Ulster settlers in the American Colonies. It was on the edge of the frontier in those days, but the settlement was successful despite the danger from hostile Indians. The records of these Marsh Creek McCains in the 1730s through the 1760s are fortunately well preserved. There are wills, court records, land and tax records. The McCains that were living there are in the Crown Colonial Records and were in the circle of several of Colonial Pennsylvania's VIPs, such as Rev. Thomas Barton, the Hamiltons, and Thomas Penn who was the son of William Penn. Rev. Thomas Barton was a prominent Anglican clergyman who presided at several weddings between McCains and Hamiltons prior to the Revolutionary War. The Hamiltons were, and still are, a family of epic accomplishments, both here and in Ireland.

In 1736, the Penn family purchased an enormous tract of land lying west of the Susquehanna from the Indians. There was a problem however, as Ulster settlers already lived on these lands and after the purchase even more of them moved into the area. This tract of land included the Marsh Creek Settlement where a growing number of McCain families lived. The Ulster folk had been hunting, trapping, and farming this land for several years. It was good land with gently rolling hills, cool clear streams, and sweeping valleys of dark fertile soil. They considered it theirs. However, the Penn family had other ideas.

In 1739-40, Thomas Penn laid out, in what is now Adams County, Pennsylvania, a reservation for himself and his family. Penn called it *Manor of the Masque* after the title of an old English estate connected to his family. Thomas Penn sent surveyors to mark out the manor. Manors were created to establish organization of a geographic area. Surveying the land to create a manor would allow for taxation of the inhabitants of the manor. This was a quaint Old World custom with which the Ulster settlers were very familiar. The appearance of a surveyor let the settlers know that now, not only were they going to be taxed, but the actual ownership of their land was in question. There is an often repeated oral history among the Marsh Creek Scots-Irish descendants that this land had been promised to these Ulster folk by Thomas Penn for services rendered. Penn had wanted men that could fight; warriors to protect the settlements to the east from Indians and to civilize and improve his estates. The Penn family eventually managed to own some 25,000,000 acres.[9] The Manor of the Masque was located on a 43,500 acre tract which included the Marsh Creek Settlement. Penn was in the middle of a long struggle to survey and implement taxation of these lands. His attempt to survey his Manor in 1741 did not turn out well.

In a letter from surveyor Zachary Butcher to the Pennsylvania Governor we hear of the attempt to survey the land.

Zach. Butcher To Gov'r, Affairs At Marsh Cr., 1741

Sr:

---

[9] Howard M Jenkins ed., *Pennsylvania Colonial and Federal: A History 1608-1903,* vol.1, (Philadelphia: Pennsylvania Historical Publishing Association, 1903), 297.

I was designed about two weeks ago to have Laid out the Manor at Marsh Creek, but the Inhabitants are got into such Terms, That it is as much as a man's Life is worth to go amongst them, for they gather'd together in Companies and go in Arms every Time they Expect I am any where near there about, with full resolution to kill or cripple me, or any other person, who shall attempt to Lay out a mannor there. Yet, if the Honble Proprietor shall think fitt to order such assistance as shall withstand such unreasonable Creatures, I shall be ready and willing to prosecute the same with the utmost Endeavor, as soon as I come back from Virginia. I am going there on an urgent occasion. I am yo^rs to serve. Zach. Butcher, Dpt[10]

The authorities made a list in 1743 of the offending obstructers of the survey with a comment made about one of them:

'Wm. McLelan, Jos. Farris, **Hugh McCain**, Matw. Black, Jam. McMichill, Robt. McFarson, Wm. Black, John Fletcher Jr., Jas. Agnew (cooper), Henry McDonath, John Alexander, Moses Jenkins, Rich'd Hall, Richard Fossett, Adam Hall, John Eddy, John Eddy Jr., Edw'd Hall, Wm. Eddy, James Wilson, James Agnew, John Steen, John Johnson, John

---

[10] Samuel Hazard ed., *Pennsylvania Archives,* vol.1. (Philadelphia, 1852), 625.

Hamilton, Hugh Logan, John McWharten, Hugh Swainey, Titus Darby, Thomas Hooswick declares y^t if ye Chain be spread again he wou'd stop it, and then took ye Compass from ye Surv. Gen.'[11]

Unreasonable Creatures? The surnames of the men listed are typical Ulster Scots of Lowland and Redshank origin and they clearly exhibited characteristics of Ulstermen in the event described. On the list is Hugh McKean who had moved from Donegal Township to the Marsh Creek settlement. The Hamilton on the list was a future in-law to the McCains. Two of Hugh McKean's sons married daughters of the settlement's leader and sheriff, Hance Hamilton, brother to John Hamilton on the list above. The sons of Hugh McKean who took a shine to Hamilton women were Hugh McKean II who married Mary Hamilton and his brother Alexander who married Sarah Hamilton. One of the McKean sisters married Thomas Hamilton a son of Hance Hamilton. Hugh McKean II was the father of Hance Hamilton McCain who along with several of his grown children moved to Choctaw County, Mississippi, in the 1830s and established my line of the family.

Senator McCain's line descends from Alexander McKean who was in the Donegal Township in 1721 through his son Alexander McKean II who moved to the southern part of the Marsh Creek settlement that was in Maryland. Senator McCain's line followed a similar path to Mississippi as that of Hugh McKean's descendants. They came down the *The Great Wagon Road,* which was the main trail that ran from

---

[11] Hazard, *Pennsylvania Archives,* 635.

Pennsylvania to Georgia, transiting the Appalachian Valley. The progenitor of the Teoc McCains, William Alexander McCain, was the great, great, grandson of Alexander McKean II of Marsh Creek. William Alexander McCain of Teoc was the third cousin of the Hance Hamilton McCain who established my branch of the family in the Mississippi Hill Country.

The Hamilton McCain connections are particularly important and are part of our story in Ireland. The McCains lived on the Hamilton estates in east Donegal and, as mentioned, there are many marriages between the two families both in Ireland and the New World. This Hamilton family is prominent in Irish history and in Ulster today, so much so that I will give some background on them in the Marsh Creek settlement.

Hance Hamilton of the Marsh Creek settlement was born in Ireland around 1711. There is a considerable amount of history and lore that has been written about him in both books and on the internet, but some of the information concerning his early life is in error. Current research tells us that he arrived in the Colonies probably in the year 1729 along with at least two brothers, John and James. DNA tests of his descendants connect him to the Abercorn Hamiltons of Donegal and northwest Tyrone. By the 1740s, Hance Hamilton was the de facto leader of the Marsh Creek Settlement. He served as sheriff of York County from 1749 through 1751 and then as a commissioned officer with the Second Battalion of the Pennsylvania Regiment. Many of his letters and official correspondence still exists and he was an eloquent writer, a Latin speaker, and a well educated man. He was a leader in the Indian wars of the 1750s and his name appears often in the Pennsylvania archives and the British Crown records.

Hance Hamilton participated in the famous Kittanning Expedition in September of 1756. He was a captain and led a company of Scots-Irish from Marsh Creek settlement. Both Hugh McKean II and his brother Alexander were in the local militia and were probably in this company. Hugh McKean II was made an Ensign in the company in 1759. The Kittanning Expedition tells much about the nature of life for the McCains in the 1750s. In the eighteenth century the Kittanning Path was a major east-west Indian trail in western Pennsylvania. It provided an overland route for the Delaware, Lenape, Shawnee, and other Indians, across the Allegheny Mountains, terminating at its western end on the Allegheny River. In the 1750s, the path was used by the Indians to conduct raids against the Scots-Irish settlements on the frontier.

Two of the Delaware leaders, Tewea and Shingas, led a series of raids beginning about October 1755. Usually these war parties were comprised of Delaware and Shawnee and were often carried out with French cooperation. The Indian warriors made no distinction between combatants and non-combatants. Women and children were routinely killed and scalped and often prisoners were tortured to death. When I researched this part of the McCain story I read through a lot of primary source material that described the gruesome violence of the era. There is an account of Indians cutting off a woman's fingers and forcing her to eat them and the burning of captives alive was a common practice of the Delawares. In the politically correct academic environment today, the ferocity and brutality of the Scots-Irish are often emphasized and that of the Indians is ignored, but put into historical context, the Scots-Irish were only giving back what they had received and they were formidable warriors. The Scots-Irish community waged total war against a people who were waging total war against them. Those were difficult times for Indian and Ulster settlers alike.

Kittanning was on the western end of the path and was considered to be a safe haven by the Indians. They believed it to be completely out of reach of the Scots-Irish. However, in September of 1756, the settlers struck back. Colonel John Armstrong and the Second Battalion of the Pennsylvania Regiment, from their staging area in Fort Duquesne, travelled 40 miles through Indian territory undetected and staged a pre-dawn attack upon the Delaware Indian village of Kittanning. They destroyed substantial supplies of munitions and food, destroyed crops, and killed around fifty Delawares including one of their leaders, the infamous Tewea. The Scots-Irish loses were high, seventeen killed and nineteen missing, but some of the latter did eventually make their way back to Fort Duquesne.

The Kittanning Raid was an epic event which sent shock waves throughout the Indian nations. Prior to the raid, the Indians had considered themselves beyond the reach of the Scots-Irish. The raid shocked the Indians to their core and revealed to them their vulnerability to these frontiersmen. Revisionist historians attempt to downplay this raid, but in reality, the raid was much like the famous Doolittle raid on Tokyo in the spring of 1942. The physical damage it did to the hostile Indians was not the ultimate fruit of the raid. It was the damage that was done to the Indian psyche and morale that was important, not to mention the death of Tewea.

This violent environment of the Pennsylvania frontier in the 1750s was a factor that sent many in that generation of McCains south. Those that came into Mississippi show up in southern Virginia prior to the outbreak of the Revolutionary War. It is possible to follow most of the lines of McCains that descend from the immigrants Alexander and Hugh without too much difficulty. Many served in the Indian wars and in the Revolutionary War. By 1760, they were in the Carolinas. They were especially numerous in the Waxhaw district, North Carolina. These McCain families moved together and they often appear as witnesses on each other's legal documents.

By the late 1700s, they were in Tennessee and a decade later in the mountains of north Alabama. The descendants of the immigrants of the original Alexander and Hugh McKean arrived in Mississippi at the same time, which was in the mid-1830s when the Choctaw Indian lands became available for settlement. It was the norm with Scots-Irish families to move west together with their kith and kin of related extended families and in-laws. The same families are found living together for many decades, even centuries. Where I sit right now in the wooded hills of north Mississippi there are dozens of McCain and Hamilton families from these lines living all around me and so it is with many other Scots-Irish families in the South.

I will give some account of Hance Hamilton McCain. I do this because our branch of the McCains is not as well-known as others. We have produced no admirals, generals, or senators, as the Teoc branch have. We do have a lot of musicians, a geologist, MEd Counselor, and a writer, so we are catching up. I like to point out that when Admiral John Sydney McCain Sr. was on his flag ship in the Pacific during WW II, my father, Leslie Gordon McCain, was not too far away on the beach at Okinawa dodging bullets. Both men were there, albeit in different roles.

Hance Hamilton McCain was a typical Scots-Irish man. He was a long hunter that moved west to follow the frontier. Hance was the type who wore a fringed hunting coat and carried a flintlock rifle. Of all the ancestors I met while finding the McCains, it is perhaps he who spoke to me in the clearest voice. He was born in the Marsh Creek settlement in the Pennsylvania colony on 11 June 1763. His life and times were a whirlwind through which he saw the birth of the United States and the days of the early Republic. During the course of his life, he appeared in court several times attempting to obtain a pension for his Revolutionary war service and his affidavits provided me with remarkable insight into his life.

At the age of 17, Hance Hamilton McCain joined the militia company of Captain John Marr in Henry County, Virginia. His company was moved about and eventually was under General Gates. On 15 August 1780, the young Hance Hamilton McCain saw the elephant; that is, he was in the battle of Camden that day. This battle was a major British victory in which Lord Cornwallis entirely routed the American forces under Gates. The way Gates handled his troops is considered to be one of the worst battlefield tactical decisions made by Colonial forces throughout the entire war. Gates placed his militia, including my dear ole ancestor, in the front line against the most experienced and elite troops of the British. I can say with absolute certainty, given the fact that I am here to report this tale, that young Hance Hamilton McCain did a considerable bit of running that day, as he survived this disaster. After the battle he reenlisted for ten months under Colonel William Polk, but stayed in service for two years.

After the war Hance married, moved to the Waxhaws in the Carolinas, and lived among his cousins there. Then, in true frontiersman fashion, he became a traveler. He moved to Georgia, Tennessee, then Kentucky, and later back to Tennessee. For a barely literate man, he did leave his mark from time to time. He worked on government sponsored surveys and road crews. He had a rifle stolen by Indians and was compensated $20 for it by the Cherokee Indian Agent in 1810. A first rate rifle cost around $15 dollars at that time, so he must have had a top of the line weapon. He worked on a road crew near the east branch of Mulberry Creek, which is where the Jack Daniels' distillery is located today. Through tax and census records, he can be followed down into the hills and mountains of northern Alabama. In May of 1824, he obtained a patent for land in what is now Fayette County, Alabama. He filed his first Revolutionary War pension application in 1833. This is a sad part of his life as his applications were turned down for lack of corroboration.

I have his pension applications and the comments by those officials trying to help him and it is pitiful and sad reading. Toward the end of his life he came upon hard times and he was worn out. His children had moved into Choctaw County, Mississippi. Hance had no money and his children were hard pressed with families of their own. The spectre of poverty was everywhere. For Hance Hamilton McCain and many other men like him, it was difficult to obtain the necessary affidavits to satisfy the bureaucrats in Washington, D.C. and obtain a war service pension. For those Revolutionary War veterans that had followed the frontier west, records were spotty, communications poor, and many old comrades were dead and gone. These men had done so much, they had fought the British and the Indians and had made the path safe for others, but their government turned its back to them.

In the 1839 letter by Hance McCain's agent to the Commissioner of Pensions, Hance is described as, "truly in a poverty stricken conditions" and "under the influence of a paralytic affliction and besides this becomes so excited when talking on the subject as to render it almost impossible to get his declaration at all." The letter goes on to say, "If the Department can do anything for him, let them do it speedily as his days are fast wasting away ... were he to die today the charity of the community would have to supply him a coffin."[12] He did die a short time later on 3 January 1840 in Tallahatchie County, Mississippi. This was where Polly McCain, mother of William Alexander McCain of Teoc, lived and, I will never know for certain but I suspect, Hance Hamilton McCain was staying with his kinsmen when he died. At least I like to think this was so.

So there we are, from Ireland in 1718 to Mississippi in the 1830s. I have tried to be brief but still relate how the Mississippi McCains came into being. Besides Hance Hamilton McCain and William Alexander McCain, there were their children and cousins who also poured into the north

---

[12] Transcript of letters in author's files.

central part of Mississippi and gave rise to the various McCain branches established there. However, that is not part of this story and now I will move on to how I found the McCains in Ireland and uncovered their history.

The Beatles

From the age of 12 onward the curiosity about my Gaelic surname was a seed in me that grew. It was a gradual and organic process. I had a typical Southern childhood. Like my peers, I had one foot in Southern suburbia and one foot planted on the farms of my grandparents. I was born in Jackson, Mississippi. When I was very young my father took a job with United Gas Pipeline Company in Ouachita Parish, Louisiana, and there I grew up and went to school. We lived on McCain Drive in Lakeshore subdivision, just outside Monroe, Louisiana. The road is named after Admiral John Sydney McCain Sr., the grandfather of Senator John McCain. My paternal grandfather had a farm in Madison County and my maternal grandfather had a farm in southern Hinds County, both in Mississippi. I spent many happy hours visiting the rural world of my grandparents and life in Ouachita Parish was also good. Like many who grew up in Louisiana, I duck hunted and fished and duck hunted some more.

Mentioning Ouachita Parish and duck hunting, I should also mention my brother and I ran in the same circles as did the now famous Robertsons of Duck Commander and Duck Dynasty fame. My brother was a star quarterback at Ouachita High School in the mid-1960s and took the field against Terry Bradshaw, another famous north Louisianan, who went on to win four Super Bowls with the Pittsburgh Steelers. I met Phil Robertson recently and, after hearing my surname, he asked me if I was of *that* McCain family that beat Terry Bradshaw and his Woodlawn High School Knights in 1965? Yes, my brother Ron and the Ouachita Parish High School Lions did beat the much favored Bradshaw led team that year 26 to 20. The Lions scored with eight seconds left and spoiled Woodlawn's homecoming. Phil Robertson, another north Louisiana man, remembered the game better than I did, but he would have as he was also a star high school football player at that time. Phil went on to play college ball at Louisiana Tech as quarterback, where Terry Bradshaw was his backup quarterback.

It was a good life in north Louisiana and typically Southern. I enjoyed a green world that Dylan Thomas could give justice to in written word. There were long trips on country gravel roads to visit kin and in-laws, nights going to sleep covered with granny made quilts and the warm magic glow of oak wood burning on the hearth. I rode mules, drove tractors, and picked berries. Then my world began to change. In the fall of 1963, in choir class at Ouachita Junior High School, I saw a group of my friends huddled around a small black box, a transistor radio. From this radio I first heard the Beatles.

After my discovery of my Gaelic surname, my next memory of ethnic self-awareness was watching *A Hard Day's Night* a year or so later in 1964. There is a subplot in the film which alludes to the Beatles' Irish roots and the tensions between the people of the north and west of the British Isles, that is their *Northerners*, and the English of the Home Counties, their *Southerners*. As I later heard a British politician put it once, "Your South is our North." He referred to the American "South," as to him it was the same as the British "North." He was quite correct. This is because the American South was settled by the Celtic fringe of the British Isles or their "Northerners." The root stock of the South is the Irish, Scots, Welsh, and Border English, who settled early and formed the society there. It is not Anglo-Saxon. It is Anglo-Celtic. As I watched the film I was fascinated by this subplot. I felt connected to the lads from Liverpool who were Irish, Ulster Scots, Welsh, and Border English in ancestry. These are subtle matters that delve into the complex history of the marginalized Celtic population in Ireland and Britain and diaspora and a type of supra-ethnicity beyond the tribal designations of Irish or Scottish, or Unionist or Nationalist, or Protestant or Catholic.

Being exposed to this *other* Britain was stimulating. In my mid-teens I had a growing yearning, much like an instinct kicking in, to go back and find the McCains in the Isles and to visit the old sod and my people. It was something I would think on and day dream about. But then the rest of the 60s happened to me and I was gone, swept away with the longhaired zeitgeist of the day, at least for a while. I made trips to Taos, New Mexico, and Telluride, Colorado, sleeping in my pickup truck, playing guitars around campfires and living in the curious half-caste world of the Southern hippie. Eventually, among a few of us survivors of *Freakdom*, some maturity kicked in, as it must when one gets older. I moved back to Mississippi and my thoughts returned to the *Macs and Os.* I began to read everything I could lay my hands on about them.

I picked up the trail of the McCains in earnest again in the mid-1970s. I did so with a much better understanding of the *Macs and Os.* I had begun the process of self-education about the history of the Celtic parts of the Isles. I knew that Gaelic could mean Irish, Scottish, or Manx. I had started the slow and laborious task of pre-internet era research. I asked my grandfather about our origins. He was born in 1890 and for this reason I hoped he had some insight or just basic knowledge about the origins of the McCains. He did not have much to say about our early history. He did tell me we were Scottish and we were kin to all the McCains in Carroll, Choctaw, Montgomery, and Webster Counties. A Scottish origin was plausible of course, but also vague and gave me no details. There was no village or township I could visit, no McCain from the old country I could call on the phone to see how their end of the family had made out these last few hundred years. I basically knew nothing other than I had a Gaelic surname.

In the mid-1970s I began to communicate with Dr. William D McCain. He was a distinguished historian from Mississippi and had served for many years as the president of the University of Southern Mississippi. He also served as president of the Sons of Confederate Veterans for many years. He was a Webster County McCain and we knew we were cousins, but not exactly sure about the details. Dr. McCain was interested in finding our history and origins. He wrote several genealogy books on branches of the McCain family from the

44

Colonial times to the present. His research confirmed by way of several old letters that the Mississippi McCains came from Ireland. The letters said we were from Ulster and mentioned places like Londonderry and County Antrim.

That was the first I knew of Ulster being part of our history. Knowing that our family came from Ulster fascinated me because of its rich history. I now had a place to focus my search. The Ulster people that came to the New World in the eighteenth century have a different sense of Irishness, or ethnicity, than an Irishman who immigrated during the Famine or later. I had discovered I had Irish roots, but I had no sense of closeness to the cultural icons of the urban Irish of the northern USA. Green beer on St Patrick's Day or the singing of the Dubliners did not speak much to me. Yet at the same time I began to perceive that there was something deeper and older in Ireland to which I was drawn.

Dr. McCain was frustrated at not being able to find any information on the McCain origins other than surname book histories which had been grafted onto our story. He suspected that there was much more to our origins. I followed his lead and began to contact as many of our kin that I could locate. Unfortunately, I found no consensus of opinion among the McCains about our origins. Many of the families knew they were from Ireland, but when asked about the origins of the family there was no clear idea. It seemed no one remembered. The McCain families I contacted offered generic information about our origins, the type found in those mass market surname books. These books usually say the surname McCain is linked to two families that belonged to Clan Donald of Argyll, Scotland. They were the McCains of Glencoe and their cousins the McCains of Ardnamurchan. The McCains of Glencoe are a romantic family best known for having suffered through the infamous Glencoe Massacre in 1692. Many years later, I would actually locate both of these McCain families when I created the McCain DNA Project.

I shared Dr. McCain's frustration of not being able to find any information about the true history of our family. I approached the research from a Mississippi McCain perspective as I had no idea at that time that we had branches of the family in New England and Canada, not to mention the many others scattered around the United States. This was over two decades before the McCain DNA Project revealed to me that the New England McKeens and the New Brunswick McCains were the same family as the Mississippi McCains. And so the research stalled with nowhere to go in the mid-1970s. But then, as unlikely as it sounds, it was a Breton living in Dublin who became the catalyst for me stepping on the path that would lead me to find the McCains.

The Breton

By 1978, I was at a dead end with my McCain research, but then fate stepped in via a friendship I formed with a fascinating man. I started corresponding with a Breton gentleman named Alan Heusaff who lived in north Dublin. He was the president of *An Conradh Ceilteach* (The Celtic League). In the late 1970s, the Celtic nations were in the news due to growing nationalist sentiments. In Scotland and Wales there was talk of self-government and devolution. The American media loved it all, not that they understood it of course. Alan Heusaff was making the international news because of his work to promote Celtic nationalism. I had seen him in a national magazine, like *Time* or *Newsweek*, I do not recall which one. He seemed to me to be someone knowledgeable about Gaelic matters. I managed to find his address and, from my house in Mississippi, I penned my first letter to him. It must have struck Alan Heusaff just a little odd to get a letter from Mississippi, but then again maybe not given his life and times. We went on to exchange many letters and developed a friendship that lasted until his passing in November of 1999.

Alan was born in Brittany in 1921 and was active in Breton cultural movements as a youth, eventually joining the *Parti National Breton* (Breton National Party) in 1938. As the war in Europe developed his involvement escalated into membership in the *Beyen Perrot*, the military wing of the party. After the German takeover of France, the *Beyen Perrot* became a unit in the German Waffen SS. This practice was not unusual and many non-Germans who fought on their side during the war were formed into units of the Waffen SS, which was part of the German military. Alan was not a political national socialist or Nazi, that is to say, nor were most of the men that joined these military units. It was just the war and doing what you thought was best at the time. Alan Heusaff saw front line service on the losing side of a war. He received the German wounded medal and achieved the rank of *Hauptsscharführer*. As you might imagine, this did not please the French authorities as they regained control. Alan Heusaff was sentenced to death *in absentia*. The full details are not all known to me, but Alan Heusaff spent the last few weeks of the war fighting his way to the Americans so he could surrender to them rather than to the French or Russians. He became a prisoner and after the war ended the French authorities tried their best to execute him, but he somehow managed to escape to Ireland on a coal ship and there he was granted asylum.[13] I heard a rumor that Otto Skorzeny was somehow involved, but I cannot substantiate this. Alan settled in Dublin and started a new life.

---

[13] George Broderick, "The Breton Movement and the German Occupation 1940-44: Alan Heusaff and Bezen Perrot: A Case-Study" (PhD diss., University of Mannheim, 2005).

There was a cadre of Breton nationalists living in Dublin after the war and most with a background similar to Alan Heusaff. In 1953, Alan married a beautiful young woman from the Donegal Gaeltacht (Gaelic speaking area), Bríd Ní Dhochartaigh. After some university study, he joined the Irish Meteorological service and remained there until his retirement. He was one of the weathermen at Dublin airport. The small Breton community in Dublin became a catalyst for pan Celtic activities and organizations in the 1950s and 1960s. In 1961, several of the Celtic political groups were brought together with the formation of the Celtic League at Rhosllannerchrugog in Wales. Alan Heusaff was a founder and the first Secretary General of the League and remained in that role for twenty-five years. Notable past and present members of the Celtic League have been Plaid Cymru's Gwynfor Evans, historian Peter Berresford Ellis, writer Bernard Le Nail, Manx language revivalist Brian Stowell, and Robert McIntyre and Rob Gibson of the Scottish National Party.

After a couple of years of exchanging letters with Alan, he suggested that I come to Dublin to stay awhile and to experience Celtic culture. I knew this was my next step so I went. With very little money, I made my way to the airport in Jackson, Mississippi, for my first trip across the big water. My girlfriend travelled with me and we had a good omen walking up to the doors of the airport. We found a 50 dollar bill in the parking lot, which in 1978 actually was some money and we were desperately short of funds. We landed at Gatwick Airport outside of London and began to hitchhike west on what became a magical and very Celtic mystery tour. I was a sight at the time, long blond hair and reddish beard, dressed in Southern style overalls and brogans, rucksack on my back in which I had a set of bag pipes which I almost could play. We drifted west, taking in many of the great sights such as Stonehenge and the Uffington White Horse. We travelled just generally west to wherever the rides were going that day and eventually we arrived at Taunton, in Somerset. Somerset to this day is one of my favorite places on this green earth.

In Taunton, I met a very generous Welshman in a pub. I was standing there ordering a pint of the best bitter and Terry, the Welshman, heard my accent. Upon finding out I was from Mississippi, he insisted my girlfriend and I stay several nights with him and his wife. He loved Mississippians, and why? Elvis Presley of course. To him, any man from Mississippi was a welcomed and honored guest in his home. Terry and I stayed up late into the night talking. He told me of his life in Wales and his desire that Wales be an independent nation. My stay with Terry was also an interesting introduction to life in the West Country. I enjoyed walks in the Quantocks hills, pints of cider, and immersion in West Country culture from some of Terry's friends who were locals. The quiet beauty of hills, woods, apple orchards, and slow moving rivers dotted with fly fishermen reminded me of Tolkien's Shire as Taunton and the surrounding country side are exactly what that brilliant writer had in mind for his Shire. Later in life, I became a reader of Evelyn Waugh. His home was located at Combe Florey in the Quantocks just to the north of Taunton. My memories of the lands around his home enriched my appreciation of his work.

My goal was to reach Dublin and Alan Heusaff so, after a week with my Welshman, it was back to the motorway to hitch a ride to south Wales and catch the ferry over to Ireland.

Hitchhiking proved to be very easy for me as I had with me a large Confederate flag. In those simpler and less politically sensitive times, the flag proved to be pure magic at getting a lift. I only had to unfurl the flag and several cars would stop in a matter of minutes to offer a ride. Tourists, especially German and Japanese, would even stop to take photographs. It was an interesting experience for a young Mississippian.

We went from Taunton to Wales and after an adventure or two in the mountains of south Wales with a slightly mad Yorkshire lorry driver we reached Swansea. We arrived around noon and had some time to kill before the ferry to Ireland left. I was learning the art of the pub so we retreated to a working class pub not too far from the docks to wait on the ferry. As was often the case on this trip, our countenance and speech became a point of interest to the locals and soon several men came over to talk to us. As fate would have it, in the pub I selected there was a black man whose father was a Mississippian. His father was a successful boxer that had settled in south Wales many years ago. The son was also a boxer which became important later that day. Now, the fact that we were from Mississippi elevated my girlfriend and I to guest of honor status and we could not buy our own beer that day in Swansea. The boxer and his mates kept us supplied in food and drink all afternoon.

We were all sitting there having a good time when a local group of socialist students came into the pub to hand out flyers promoting what they were calling a workers rally. Word got around within their group that there were two Mississippians seated in the pub and being good socialists they decided to accost us for the many sins that their pea-brains imagined all white Mississippians to be guilty. They got in our faces, you might say. The students were doing this at the precise moment when the black gentleman had just asked to see the Confederate flag I carried in my rucksack. Picture, if you will, a group of unwashed socialist students accosting two young, thin Mississippians showing a black boxer a Confederate flag. It was just too good. This was the sort of thing I could not make up if I tried.

In addition to the black boxer, there had gathered a group of older men, mostly WW II vets around us. We were all having a great time and the excellent Welsh ale was flowing while the Confederate flag was waving. The Confederate battle flag was a proverbial red flag in front of the bull to the socialist students and they turned up their rhetoric. I was deciding which one I was going to drop first when the black boxer grew agitated and sprang into action. He forcibly ushered the socialist students out with the parting command to not come back and if they did they would be smashed. He returned to the pub, apologized for the rude students, and proceeded to buy us more ale than we could ever drink.

A couple of hours after the pub incident we wandered down to the docks to board the ocean going ferry, a little tipsy, but I remember it well as it was there I first heard Gaelic being spoken in a natural setting. There was a small group of young men in the queue ahead of us waiting to board the ferry to Cork. They were speaking to each other in Gaelic and I knew enough of the language to recognize what they were sayimg. I approached and greeted them in what little Gaelic I had learned from books. They were shocked but entirely delighted to hear a pilgrim from Dixie greet them in their own tongue. There were also Welsh speakers making the voyage over to Cork and this made my first exposure to the old languages a rich one. I arrived in Cork after a night time passage across the Irish Sea. It was a magic voyage on a clear night and I walked up on the deck to look at the moon's reflection upon the Celtic Sea. I was a New World Gael on the ramble in the old country.

My travel companion and I had no trouble at all hitchhiking north from Cork and by late afternoon on the day of our arrival we were being dropped off at O'Connell Street in the center of Dublin. We were standing on the O'Connell street sidewalk, looking a bit dazed and confused, when a weathered old man on a bicycle pedaled up to us and asked if we needed a place to stay. Whether it was synchronicity, fate, or old gods, I cannot say, but the old man set me on a path that placed me into the Gaelic subculture in Dublin within minutes of my arrival there. The man directed us to a youth hostel on Frenchman's Lane and one of the first people I spoke to in the hostel was a young man from the west of Ireland. He was staying in the youth hostel while he tried to find work in Dublin. The young man was a Gaelic speaker and when he discovered we were interested in the Gaelic world he immediately, that night, took us to *An Club*, a small Irish speaking pub under the Conradh Na Gaeilge (The Gaelic League) building in Dublin. There I met Gaelic speakers from Kerry, Connemara, and Donegal, and even a few from the Hebrides, who would wander in late at night for the *craic*.[14] It was a rich environment of strong Irish pipe tobacco smoke mixed with the smell of wet wool, Guinness, and old wood.

---

[14] A Gaelic word meaning, good conversation, drink, music, laughter and song.

Every atom of the place was permeated with Gaelicness and I soaked it up the way only a Mississippian could. For several months, I spent many nights in *An Club,* often sitting there into the wee hours of the morning, just listening to Gaelic being spoken and learning about this Ireland.

I met with Alan and Bríd Heusaff after a couple of days in Dublin and had dinner at their house. I had the opinion Alan was interested in me because I did not have the background of the Irish Americans he knew. I was a type of American he was not familiar with, a Southerner, and my views and politics were different than those of the Irish Americans he knew from New York or Chicago. He had fought in a war against the United States as had my own ancestors in Mississippi and that alone gave us some common ground. Alan was a busy man but managed to take me to those places in Dublin where Gaelic was spoken and introduced me to a world that would have been hard to find without his help. Alan Heusaff arranged for us to stay at his daughter's house in Dublin and I learned the ebb and flow of the old city while staying there. This was way before the Celtic Tiger. This was a Dublin where you could still hear Irish spoken in the streets and you could still see a horse and cart occasionally and beggars too. Dubliners were slender back then and they had less money, but dressed much better and seemed to be a happy people. In the 1978 version of Dublin, you could feed yourself on rich Irish milk and chips for under 10 pence.

I have so many memories of my first stay in Dublin. One day I was in St Stephen's Green and saw an elderly man in a green uniform. He was a veteran of the 1916 Easter Rising. A crowd of people were around him in gentle conversation and

I knew I was seeing a piece of history. To read about events in history is one thing, but to see them sitting in front of you gives life to that history. On this trip, I was introduced to Seán Mac Stiofáin, who had been the chief of staff with the IRA in the early 1970s. When I met him, I was oblivious to his background. I found him an interesting man, intelligent and well-read. By the time I met him, he was out of the IRA business. I later found out he was of Protestant Irish ancestry. After he retired from politics, his main interest was promoting Gaelic language. When I was introduced to him, he was in a street market where he had a little table out on which he sold Irish language books. We had tea and McVities and a conversation. Like Alan, he was interested in meeting a *Southerner*. He told me about John Mitchell, a famous Presbyterian Irish nationalist from County Londonderry, who lived in the nineteenth century and who was also a great champion of the Southern Confederacy. Two of John Mitchell's sons were killed in action in the Confederate army.

A few days after meeting Mac Stiofáin, I was almost stoned to death, which I can tell you gets a lad's attention. I remember the date, it was 20 September 1978, a date easy to remember as it was the day the Irish national football team, or soccer that is, played the Northern Irish squad in Dublin. I have never developed an interest in soccer, but many people do in that part of the world and this game was an extreme grudge match, not so much for the players, but rather for the fans. It was Irish republicanism versus Northern Irish Unionism on the football pitch to them. It was proxy war for many of the people who went to see the match that day. Some 46,000 fans packed into Lansdowne Road to see the first ever meeting between the two teams. Like most soccer games, the actual game was a dour anti-climax with the stunning score of 0-0. But, after the game, a throng of Dubliners decided it would be a great idea to break all the windows out of the tour busses that carried the many Northern Irish fans to the match, which is where I came in. I was walking in Dublin that day. If memory serves, I was near Merrion Square, and it might have been on Merrion Square South road. I was walking and minding my own business. Now, for all the world, I looked like a native Dubliner circa 1978. I had long blond hair and long red beard. I was wearing blue jeans and an Irish wool sweater over my shirt. It was the look of a hard core Jackeen in those days. I was walking to meet someone to study Gaelic when to my astonishment a long procession of tour buses began to slowly drive by me. More than that, these buses had most of the windows smashed and the men inside were angry, loud, and had stones and broken pieces of brick in their hands and were just looking for someone to clobber. Their collective eyes fell upon this tall, lanky, young man, from Mississippi. I stopped and looked at them and immediately realized I was in a tight spot. I suppose the buses were seeking a way out of Dublin that would lead to no more incoming rounds. Whatever the case, it was not a good situation for me. I literally expected a brick to smash into my head at any second. I said nothing to them, just turned back around and continued walking down the sidewalk to their jeers and cat calls. Most were unintelligible to me, so I was not particularly offended. The buses had been moving very slow, but at this time they picked up a little speed and soon they were moving past me. No brick came, but I knew I had barely escaped being drawn into a nasty incident and, me, just a pilgrim from Mississippi.

Another memory from this trip was a mad drive across Ireland from Dublin to An Cheathrú Rua, which is west of Galway, in a three cylinder Renault (it had four, but one wasn't working). While on this dash, there was a moment in the Irish midlands when twin brilliant rainbows appeared across the sky as we travelled. It is so vivid in my memory, I can close my eyes and see them perfectly right now. Ireland tends to provide people with memories like that.

An Cheathrú Rua is in the Connemara Gaeltacht and my first visit there had a profound effect upon me. In the 1970s, there were still plenty of old timers there, even a few Gaelic monoglots, dressed in their conservative black clothing, speaking their Gaelic, smoking pipes and drinking Guinness. In the fall of 1978, there were few vacation homes in sight, no 300,000 Euro homes with all modcoms, no crowds of tourists invading the place, just the old Gaeltacht. I fell totally in love with the place, a love that continues to this day. To walk along the path in the village of An Cheathrú Rua, to smell the turf fires burning on the hearths, to sit in a quiet pub and have a pint of Guinness while the Irish language is being spoken around me, well, that is my heaven. I remember the first time I gathered up my courage and addressed a native speaker in Irish. It was an elderly couple I met on the sidewalk. We exchanged greetings, and I chanced a comment about the weather, which they understood and they made a speculative reply about tomorrow's weather. That conversation is one of the great memories of my life. I have been to the Irish Gaeltachtaí (plural of Gaeltacht) many times since that first visit and the changes that have taken place there in the last four decades are profound. I am pleased I had the chance to visit there in 1978 to see it before the changes.

Alan Heusaff taught me my first real Irish. He was very good with languages. His native language was Breton, but he also knew French, and German, and then he learned Irish and was fluent. The last language he learned was Welsh. Alan himself would occasionally come to *An Club*. People would sometimes hint at his colorful past. But, there were plenty of WW II veterans around in those days and in Europe, understandably, and many had served in the German or Italian armies. Alan's passion in life was gardening and he was a master at it. After he retired from his work in Dublin, he moved to the Connemara Gaeltacht where he lived until he passed away in 1999. He was an amazing man and he is missed. He was an intelligent man, a sublime Celt, a friend, and a gentleman in every regard. Sitting here now, I can say that, if he had not introduced me to the Gaelic world of today, I would have never found my McCains.

My first trip to Ireland was followed by many more though strangely enough I did not delve deeply into the origins of the McCains for the next few years. For the time being, I was content to have reconnected with a Gaelic world. I had no idea it was still around as the books I had read exaggerated its demise. It was there, still alive and vibrant, even if it was a sub-culture by the time I found it. I travelled several times to An Cheathrú Rua and would go out to Inis Mór. I also travelled to the Scottish Highlands and to the Isle of Man.

Traveling to Ireland was always fun and eventful. During one trip I met Muhammad Ali. It was 11 September 1984. I was flying out of Newark, New Jersey, to Shannon, in County Clare, Ireland. I had an hour or so to kill so was just sitting in the waiting area of my loading gate. I noticed an athletic black man come into the area and take a seat. Now, I recognized him immediately. It was Muhammad Ali and do not ask how I knew. In my age group, one knows Muhammad Ali. I had seen him on television many times dating back to the mid-1960s. He was iconic to say the least. I was a fan of his, had always pulled for him in his bouts. I liked his style in the ring and also his rebel spirit. I was intrigued that he was by himself. I got up from where I was sitting, walked over and sat down beside him and said, "Hello Muhammad, what brings you here."

I am six foot two inches and fairly well built, so I was not overly impressed with his size, but I did notice the easy way he moved, the way athletes move, fluid and with power. There were introductions and we talked. I told Muhammad I was a native born Mississippian, to which he smiled broadly. This grew into a conversation about ethnicity, the War Between the States, race relations in the North, in the South, things in Ireland, etc. Muhammad was friendly, talkative, and liked my upfront casual nature with my Southernness. He told me he had great respect for white Southern males. In his dealings with Southern white men, Muhammad found them to be straight forward and honest. He was interested in my travel to Ireland as I told him I was hunting for ancestors. We also had fun talking about the pilot, who was female. When I was checking in, the airline people told me this was the first trans-Atlantic flight to be piloted by a woman. For some reason they wanted me to know. Muhammad made some good natured, humorous remarks about our upcoming flight and female pilot. We had about twenty minutes to talk and were having a very good time. Then the local airport security realized they had a major celebrity in their midst. A guard appeared, then two, then several of Muhammad's entourage came up. I suppose they had been checking luggage or something. Within another five minutes around twenty people were gathered around him. Within thirty minutes there were near a hundred as word got out that he was there. After that, it was no longer possible to talk to him and I wished him well and got up to leave. Then, for some reason, I decided to ask him for an autograph just to prove to others the conversation had taken place. As a rule, I do not ask autographs from famous people I meet, but I did this time. I later found out that he was going to Dublin to consult with doctors about what would be diagnosed as Parkinson's syndrome and he would never fight again.

In 1984, having a Gaelic surname could cause travel complications. On my 1984 trip, not only did I meet Muhammad Ali, but I was also questioned by United States security "agents" when I returned back to the USA. On 12 October, the IRA had planted a bomb in the Grand Hotel in Brighton, England because the Conservative Party conference was being held there. Their target was Margaret Thatcher. Prime Minister Thatcher narrowly escaped injury, but five people were killed, including two high-profile members of the Conservative Party, and 31 people were injured. It was bloody business. In September 1985, IRA man Patrick Magee was found guilty of planting the bomb, detonating it, and of five counts of murder. Magee received eight life sentences. The judge recommended that he serve at least 35 years. Later, Home Secretary Michael Howard lengthened this to "whole life." However, Magee was released from prison in 1999 under the terms of the Good Friday Agreement and did only 14 years of his sentence.

I was making the return flight to the USA in early November of 1984. Security was understandably heightened. Macs and Os doing unusual things on international flights were suspect. I was making a connecting flight between Aer Lingus and Delta back in Newark and was running late. Aer Lingus, being the sports they used to be, whisked me through customs by some semi-secret door and, presto, I was making my way toward the Delta aircraft. Then "security" caught up with me. It was Federal agents, I forget the brand name, but they had guns and the whole business. You see, the IRA bombers were thought to be leaving the UK and trying to make for the USA. Then, here comes this man named Barry McCain (a suspicious sounding name) that is being allowed to go around the customs station and placed directly on his flight.

Well, the Federal agents were expecting a hard core IRA man, but instead got an educated Mississippi Redneck of Gaelic ancestry. The interrogation should have been taped as it was not without its points of humor. Back then there were occasionally clever people working as Federal agents. It took the older man with gray highlights in his thinning hair about thirty seconds to realize exactly who and what I was. He began to grin. Now, the younger ones, full of piss and vinegar, were not ready to give it up, but gray hair trumps. He allowed me to pass and even helped me get to my plane in time.

In the 1980s, I gradually began to think about the McCains and their origins and trying to find them in Ireland again. Dr. William McCain and I continued to communicate. He was interested in my travels and my interest in Gaelic language and culture. He knew, as did I, that our family had its origins in that Gaelic world. We both thought the story of the

McCains being Highland Scots from Clan Donald to be plausible. Perhaps we could find a primary source that would support this theory. This was, after all, the most widely circulated origin myth and I had no reason to question it. I had read enough on the subject to know that there had been large numbers of Argyll and Hebridean Gaels who had moved to Ireland to assist the Irish in their wars against the Normans and later the English. There was a hereditary Scottish warrior caste called the *Gallóglaigh* that migrated to Ireland in medieval times and several well-known Irish clans are of this origin. In the 1500s, more Scottish Gaels, called Redshanks, came into Ulster. Redshank surnames are found all across Ulster to this day. Dr. McCain and I believed that the McCains would fit somewhere within the Gallóglaigh or Redshanks story.

In the 1980s, I went to Ole Miss and received a history degree and put my research skills to work. I poured through old records and found dozens of McCain families in Ireland, Scotland, and the Isle of Man, but it seemed an impossible task to sort them out and certainly no way to discern to which one we belonged. There were more trips to Ireland and Scotland, but no progress made in finding the McCains. Then, in the 1990s, computers and the internet came into my life. With these new tools, I found my milieu and the hunt for the McCains heated up. The game was afoot.

Back On the Path

In 1997, I went online and started searching for information on McCains using this new research tool. I found websites that offered histories of our family and there were several versions of the story. I posted my opinion of the facts as I understood them and emails were exchanged. Because of my travels in Ireland, my degree in history, and my knowledge of Gaelic, several McCains asked me to see if we had relatives still living in Ireland, to contact them and to discover our origins and put the matter to rest once and for all. I found myself back in the hunt for the McCains. Dr. William McCain had confirmed that we did at least have connections to north County Antrim, Ireland. From the perspective of my Mississippi McCains, Antrim, which is now in Northern Ireland, seemed the obvious place to begin the search anew.

North Antrim is the cusp of the two Gaelic worlds of Ireland and Scotland. Antrim history includes Highland Scots and Hebrideans that moved back and forth between Ireland and Scotland. I believed that was relevant to the McCains. When you stand on the shore near Ballintoy in north Antrim you can look out and see the Hebridean island of Islay. If you go east just a few miles into the Glens of Antrim and look to the east across the twelve short miles of sea, you will see the coast line of Kintyre in Scotland. In centuries past, when the English made incursions into Antrim, the Gaels of the Glens would light signal fires from the tops of the coastal mountains to call for help from the Gaels a short distance away in Kintyre. The Scottish Clan Donald ruled the Glens and later The Route, the district west of the Glens, for hundreds of years.

Encouraged by the ease at which the internet allowed me to research, I renewed my hunt for the McCains under the assumption that we were a Highland Scots family who had come to Antrim from the Hebrides or west Highlands. I researched every Gaelic extended family that used the anglicized name McCain in north Antrim. However, I ran into an interesting situation, not that I could not find McCains, but rather that there were too many of them. It is a land inundated with surnames of Cain, O'Kane, and McCain, in a bewildering variety of anglicized forms. It is the epicenter for Gaelic surnames of the Cain brand and an onomastic labyrinth. Despite the obvious connections of the surname McCain to north Antrim, I had no way of distinguishing between the various Cain families there. I succeeded in learning volumes about branches of the Clan Donald and discovered they had a half dozen families surnamed McCain. Anyone of them could have migrated to north Antrim. The problem was there was no way to confirm if any of these McCain families had connections to my Mississippi McCains.

It was at this time I met Austin Rock, a native Dubliner, who had an interest in Gaelic families and clans. He spent hours collecting information from dusty library shelves in Dublin about dozens of McCain families that were connected to north Antrim. Hundreds of emails passed between Oxford, Mississippi, and north Dublin, fuelled by liberal quantities of Jameson and cups of coffee. Often my email subject line would read *the McCain Pain*. This was because of the sheer insanity of trying to find one McCain needle in a McCain haystack. Not only that, Austin and I discovered that some of the O'Kane families in north Antrim had also anglicized their surname as McCain, so we not only had to track the many Hebridean and Highland McCains, but also the native Irish McCains. It was a Gordian knot of seemingly insurmountable complexity.

I remember getting an email from Cindy McCain, wife of Senator John McCain. Undoubtedly she was helping the Senator with research on his book *Faith of Our Fathers*. I answered her email inquiry as best I could, recounting the fact that north Antrim was full of Highland Scots and that indeed some McDonalds did use the surname McCain, and as best I knew we could be one of them. But, I had not yet found any records to support that history and I knew we could just as easily be a branch of the O'Kane family.

The O'Kane family in north Antrim is a branch of the County Derry O'Kane family from the Dungiven area. The north Antrim family includes the famous Manus Rua O'Kane, who was a colonel under Montrose in the Wars of the Three Kingdoms. The Wars of the Three Kingdoms were an intertwined series of conflicts that took place in England, Ireland, and Scotland between 1639 and 1651. Part of these wars was a general Irish Rising and north Antrim was the site of several epic battles. I found records that McCains participated in these battles on the Irish side, but many of the

Irish troops were actually Scots from the Isles and Argyll. Manus Rua O'Kane and Montrose enjoyed a series of dramatic victories in Scotland, which came to an end at the battle of Philiphaugh in September of 1645. Montrose's troops were defeated and Manus Ó Rua Catháin surrendered and was granted quarter, but then treacherously hung. His sons survived the wars and lived in north Antrim around Ballintoy and Ballinlea. They converted to the Protestant faith and some of them used the surname McCain. Could my McCains be some of his descendants?

In 2000, I decided to travel to Northern Ireland in the hope that being there, in north Antrim, talking with the locals, looking at the places that I knew McCains had lived, that I might just uncover something. I had been to Ireland many times, but this was my first journey into the six counties of Northern Ireland. The beauty of Northern Ireland was inspiring but it was also my introduction to *The Troubles* and the weight of Ulster history. You would think that a Mississippian whose family has been in the New World for 289 years would not be drawn into the sectarian aspects of Ulster history and the continuing conflicts there, however, this is not the case. In the six counties, history and especially family history carries with it baggage. In some places I saw the tell-tale signs of a divided society, the flags and graffiti, the guarded talk, the veiled questions trying to ascertain one's loyalties or religion. I was prying and asking questions. I needed to go back into the past, which in Ulster opens a door to passionate feelings and loyalties. This is in contrast to the Irish Republic. It was a new experience for me.

In County Antrim, I went to Bushmills, Ballintoy, Ballinlea, and Ballycastle. I found the local historians and talked with them about McCain families. They knew surprisingly little, but some did say they thought the local McCains had been the descendants of Manus Rua O'Kane. One of the places associated with this O'Kane family is the ruined ancient church of Templastragh, which I found sitting in the middle of a farmer's field, not far from the sea. Right in the middle of the ruin is a McCain grave, or graves really, one stone, but two graves. The stone reads:

> Here lyeth the Body of
> Cathrine McCain
> who departed this
> life th 9th of November 1811
> Aged 61 years wife to
> William McCain
> Late of Bushmills who
> Departed this life ye
> 17th of March in the year
> 1813 Aged 70 years[15]

That was at least encouraging and seemed to point toward O'Kane origins for us, but if so the oral history of the Teoc McCains was wrong. I also visited Dunseverick castle, or the ruin of it, as only one tower is left standing. The O'Kane family made a last ditch stand there against Cromwell's juggernaut. The O'Kanes lost and Cromwell's engineers filled

---

[15] Francis Joseph Bigger and William J Fennell, "Teampull Lastrach, Dunseveric, Co Antrim," *Ulster Journal of Archaeology*, vol. 5 (Belfast: The Linenhall Press, 1899): 60-1.

the castle with black powder and touched it off. What you see today is the results. The castle is a dramatic vista, even in total ruins as it is. Dunseverick is a historic place for another reason. It was the Irish capital of the early medieval kingdom of Dál Riada.

I came home from my Fall 2000 trip with a new found zeal to get to the bottom of the McCain story, but with no hard facts and only the grave at Templastragh to suggest any origins for us. I was stumped, but then two things happened that proved profound; I received an email from a McCain from Ballywatt, in north Antrim and DNA testing for the purpose of genetic genealogy became available.

The email came in the summer of 2003 from Joe McKane who lives in Chattanooga, Tennessee, but he was born in Northern Ireland and was a native of the village of Ballywatt, in Ballyrashane Parish, County Antrim. Ballywatt is about four miles south southeast of the town of Bushmills. Joe McKane's family had lived in Ballywatt since the early 1700s. As I learned about Joe's family, I believed there was a connection between his family and the family buried in Templastragh. This was progress, because I knew the Mississippi McCains had a connection with north Antrim. Joe told me he had read my writings on the McCain family that I had posted on the internet and certain names of the early McCains in the Marsh Creek settlement were the same ones used with his family. Joe thought it highly likely we were cousins. Joe had emigrated from Northern Ireland to Tennessee in 1979, as he told me, because he was sick of the *Troubles*. He mentioned watching human parts being scraped off a wall after a bombing as a motivating factor. Joe did not know the origins of the McCain family. As a boy in Ireland he had never heard any definite story, but at least he was a bona fide north Antrim McCain. I also thought it likely that Joe was one of our distant Irish cousins, but had no way to prove it.

After I took my history degree from Ole Miss, I kept up with the world of history research. When DNA testing became a tool of the historian in the 1990s, I was already thinking of its application. I read about the Cheddar Man and Bryan Sykes. The Cheddar man is the name given to the skeletal remains of a man found in Gough's Cave in Cheddar Gorge, Somerset in southwest England. The remains dated to circa 7150 BC. In 1996, Bryan Sykes of Oxford University extracted some viable mitochondrial DNA from the Cheddar man. Sykes then decided to see if, by chance, any of the residents of the Cheddar village were a DNA match, that is to say, a descendant from the maternal side of the Cheddar Man. He tested the local population and found that Adrian Targett, a history teacher in the village, and two schoolchildren, were mitochondrial matches to the Cheddar Man. His direct descendants were still living within a short distance of where his remains had been found, incredible stuff. This was more than excellent and I knew it was just a matter of time until paternal DNA, or Y chromosome DNA testing, would be available. A Y chromosome DNA test would prove or disprove whether or not Joe McKane of Ballywatt and I were cousins through a paternal line.

In the autumn of 2003, both Joe McKane and I received an email from a man surnamed Keane in Massachusetts who had started a DNA Project and he wanted us to participate. We learned that this project had an agenda that both Joe and I were uncomfortable with. The man wanted to be declared Taoiseach of Clann Uí Chatháin (chief of the O'Kane clan). Despite my interest in the O'Kane family, I did not want to be involved in what could be an Irish clan power struggle. If someone wanted to claim this chieftainship that was well and good, but my interests were focused on finding my McCain cousins in Ulster and learning our history. I did not want the controversy of what is a legal matter of the Irish courts to cloud my research so I decided that I would start a McCain family DNA project of my own. A series of emails between Joe McKane and me led to the creation of the McCain DNA Project.

There are several firms that do DNA testing for individuals and groups doing genealogical research as well as research concerning ethnicity and genetic characteristics. It has developed into a huge and profitable business. I chose Family Tree DNA Ltd., whose headquarters are in Houston, Texas, because they were the most user friendly and have the largest number of participants in their data base. In 2000, Family Tree DNA was founded by Bennett Greenspan and Max Blankfeld. It was the first company dedicated to direct to the consumer DNA testing for genetic genealogy and family history research. For surname studies, the Y chromosome (Y-DNA) test is used. Surnames are handed down through the paternal line making Y-DNA testing the perfect tool for paternal ancestry research because this DNA material is only passed from father to son. For this reason only men can participate in the test. The results are classified by haplogroup and haplotype.

Haplogroups are the major branches of the Y-chromosome tree. They are defined by Single Nucleotide

Polymorphisms (SNPs) which have accumulated over many generations as the Y-chromosome is passed from father to son. These SNPs map the paths back to the single common male ancestor from which all from that group descend. Haplogroups are mainly used for anthropological and deep ancestry research because the time frames are usually prior to the adoption of surnames. Haplogroups are useful for researchers who are studying human migration patterns and have archeological value. They can also be used to study tribal groups in early European history. In layman's terms, this data can tell you if you are a Celt, Viking, Anglo-Saxon, or if your ancestors spent the last Ice Age in Iberia.

The Y-DNA haplotype is used for genetic genealogy. It deals with a more recent time frame relating to one's ancestor and all the men that descend from him during the time when surnames were coming in use. One's father, grandfather, great-grandfather and so on, all carry the same Y chromosome DNA. All the males that descend from the same forefather will have the same or very similar Y-DNA. Once a man tests his Y-DNA, all the other men that have tested who also descend from that common male ancestor will show up as a match in the DNA results. When a Y-DNA haplotype match group is located the next step is genetic genealogy.

Genetic genealogy compares the haplotypes of two or more people that are a Y-DNA match to determine the degree of genetic relationship between their respective lines. The closeness of the match, or distance, gives an indication of the time to the shared paternal ancestor. At this point, other factors become important such as having the same or similar sounding or meaning surname, or a surname's clan connections, or the geographic location of a match. All these factors help to determine if two related lines are of genealogical interest. Many families triangulate with members of their match group to fill in gaps, or *smash through brick walls,* to add to their family's genealogy and locate members of their family still in the old country. An example of this; let us say Y-DNA testing confirmed that three families, that did not previously know they were related, actually share a paternal kinship dating to circa 1700. Family A might have part of the story, and then match Family B which has more of the story, which matches Family C still in Ireland which has even more of the story. When the stories of Family A, B, and C are put together, often a complete shared family history and genealogy are revealed. In the case of many Irish and Scottish families, both surname and non-surname matches are important because surnames were not fixed until the early modern era in parts of Scotland and Ireland. Members of the same clan that share paternal ancestry may not share the same surname, but in the primary sources it is often possible to discover a group of surnames linked to a paternal line. Y-DNA haplotype testing allows primary sources from families in your match group to be used with confidence since paternal kinship has been confirmed.

The actual process of starting the project was simple. I went online to the Family Tree homepage, exchanged a few emails with their contact people and in a matter of minutes I had the McCain DNA Project up and running. Next, I ordered my DNA test via credit card and it was sent to me via the post. The test itself is also easy to do. You have two sterile cotton swabs with which you take a tissue sample from the inside of your mouth by rubbing your inner cheek. This procedure is done twice 24 hours apart. The samples are placed in sealed containers which are mailed back to the lab and some four to six weeks later you receive your results via an email message.

Joe and I both ordered our kits and waited impatiently to see the results. I had been hunting for Irish McCains for decades now and I was more than a little nervous about the results of the test. To actually confirm kinship with a McCain born and bred in Ireland would mean a lot to me. I would have at least found some of the McCains that had remained behind in Ireland. Joe had family in Northern Ireland and Dublin. If we were a match, I would have parts of our history in Ireland confirmed complete with cousins, old McCain home sites, tombstones, and more. It was now just a matter of waiting for the lab to do the test and send us the results.

Irish Cousins

I received an email from the Family Tree DNA in early November of 2003. This would be it, the answer in black and white. Either Joe McKane of Ballywatt, County Antrim was my distant cousin or he was not. I clicked on the email and opened it to read, "You have a match." Yes, I did have a match and it was to Joe McKane of Ballywatt. I had found the Irish McCains or a least some of them. This was success. I was amazed that a simple tissue sample could accomplish what I had spent many years trying to do, but I did not mind at all being outdone by a white coated geneticist. It was just good to finally locate some of the family that had remained in Ireland. I realized also that Y chromosome DNA testing was a powerful research tool for the historian and genealogist alike and that my DNA match to Joe McKane was only the beginning.

Joe and I both were pleased and relieved. The connections between his family and mine were real and proven and this was a catalyst to proceed onward. I wanted to expand the DNA project, to find more of our family. The internet allowed me to do this at a rapid pace. I put the word out on every relevant genealogy forum and message board in Ireland, Northern Ireland, and the Diaspora, that the McCain DNA

Project was up and running and needed McCain surnamed men to participate. During the months that followed the initial match between Joe McKane and me, I succeeded in recruiting McCain men for DNA testing from Australia, Canada, the USA, Ireland, Scotland, the Isle of Man, New Zealand, and the UK.

As these McCains joined the project, matches began to come in. The next McCain match was to Jim McKane of Ontario, Canada. A match in Canada was the first indication that I might have found something beyond just an Ulster family that settled in Mississippi. Jim McKane is a retired financial planner and is a significant figure in Canadian genealogical circles because of his work in the field over the years. Jim had emailed me years before with questions about my Mississippi McCains, hoping that we were related and I knew something about the family that could help his own research. Jim McKane came on board the McCain DNA Project as webmaster and also began to build a data base of each McCain family that matched our family.

The Canadian matches were significant because McCain is one of the more famous surnames in Canada and it all has to do with the Irish potatoes. In the 1820s through the 1840s there was a second Ulster Migration which was larger than the one that went into Colonial America in the previous century. This second Ulster migration went primarily to New Brunswick and Ontario, Canada. Several McCain families from the Finn Valley in Donegal settled in New Brunswick and one of these families gave rise to McCain Foods, Ltd., one of the most successful food processing firms in the world. McCain Foods was founded in 1956 by brothers Wallace and

Harrison McCain. It is a global brand with annual sales of over 6 billion dollars, operations in 15 countries, and marketed in 160 countries. One out of every three French fries eaten on planet earth comes from McCain Foods. Both Wallace and Harrison were awarded Canada's highest civilian award, the *Order of Canada* for a lifetime of outstanding achievement and service to the nation. Margaret McCain, wife of Wallace, also has the Order of Canada and was Lieutenant Governor of New Brunswick.

The DNA Project had matches to New Brunswick McCains. This was followed by more DNA matches to McCain families in Donegal as well as families that had originated in Donegal. It was a complete surprise to me that the New Brunswick McCains and the Mississippi McCains were the same family. We were from different generations of immigrants, but the same family. There were more matches in Ireland, Scotland, and across the United States. It was apparent that I had found a much larger family than I had imagined. My research started with my own family, but it was now obvious that the Mississippi McCains were but a small part of a much larger Gaelic patronymic clan. As the project continued, the geneticists improved the DNA analysis and expanded the number of loci (DNA markers) included in the test. With these refinements of the DNA results, I could tell that all these McCains, from New Brunswick, from Donegal, from Mississippi, from New England, etc., descended from a McCain family living in Ulster in the mid-1600s.

Not all was joy as I began to find our McCains. The DNA results smashed to pieces several family myths that had been attached to our history over the years. One myth was the story that we were of the ruling line of the Scottish Clan Donald. It was a romantic and colorful bit of lore and what could be better than to be vanquished Scottish Highland chiefs. There were two versions of this McDonald myth, the main one being that we were the noble McCain House of Glencoe, Argyll, Scotland, of the infamous massacre. The Massacre of Glencoe is one of the sadder tales in Scottish history. The McDonald McCain family was the ruling house of the Glencoe branch of the Clan Donald. During the era of the Glorious Revolution, they were a little late in pledging their allegiance to the new monarchs, William and Mary. Their tardiness had been carefully orchestrated by their rivals in that other great Scottish clan, the Campbells. Two companies of the Earl of Argyll's men (the Earl was the chief of the Campbells) were billeted among the McCain family of Glencoe while the family attempted to register their pledge of loyalty to the new king. By Gaelic custom, the Glencoe McCains gave their hospitality to these Campbell soldiers, despite the tension between the two clans. It was all a Campbell stratagem to gain entry into the homes of the Glencoe McCains. On the morning of 13 February 1692, the Campbell guests awoke at 5 o'clock in the morning and set upon their McCain hosts. It was brutal and bloody. Thirty-eight McCain men and in-laws were killed that morning. The Campbell soldiers burned the homes of the McDonald McCains and another forty women and children died of exposure in the extreme winter conditions.

As McCain families around the world joined our DNA Project, the Glencoe McCain families were located and were tested. When their DNA results came in, they were not a match to our McCains. It was easy to spot the Glencoe McCains as not only did they not match us, but they were a

DNA match to the McDonald chiefs, as they should have been. Finding them was something I was proud of, even though in doing so I proved we were not that famous family. They are an interesting and important part of Scottish history. It was rewarding to help these McCains confirm their ancestry. The Glencoe McCain paternal DNA is Norse, by the way, and their progenitor was a Viking. Our McCains, on the other hand, are genetically typical insular Celts.

The other Clan Donald lore came from several of our McCain families that had adopted a similar story that we were yet another McDonald McCain family, the McCains of Ardnamurchan, also located in Argyll, Scotland. They also have an interesting, romantic, and equally tragic story. In the 1620s, the Campbells seized the lands of the Ardnamurchan McCains. These McCains, then, became pirates on the north Atlantic making a living by taking ships in the Hebrides until an epic battle brought them down. Not all was bad news as one branch of them finally settled on the island of Islay and started the distillery that gave rise to one of the best single malt whiskies on this planet, Laphroaig. As with the Glencoe McCains, the descendants of the Ardnamurchan McCains also joined our McCain DNA Project. The Ardnamurchan McCains' DNA results were not a match to us, but did match their paternal kin, the Glencoe McCains and the McDonald chiefs. So, I smashed another of our McCains' origin myths. We were not the Ardnamurchan McCains.

DNA results proved we were not the McDonald McCains, but still gave no clue to our origins. The basic question I wanted to answer was, were we native Irish Gaels or had we come to Ulster from someplace in Scotland? The DNA results had revealed a growing number of connections to the McCain families in east Donegal. We also had two matches from McCains living in Scotland, but both families descended from Irish immigrants from east Donegal. Both the Teoc McCains and the New England McKeens had an oral history of being linked to Scotland, yet the DNA Project had eliminated every Scottish origin McCain family that had participated in the test. I would have to take a step back and not assume any Scottish connections. I had no explanation for the east Donegal connections. On the other hand, Joe McKane's family lived close to Dunseverick, the old ancestral home of the north Antrim O'Kane family and some in this family took the surname McCain. I knew I would have to find descendants of the O'Kane family and ask them to participate in the McCain DNA Project. This was the logical next step in the research.

The O'Kane Clan

The O'Kanes are one of the more famous families in Ireland. I visited two O'Kane locations, Dunseverick Castle and Templastragh Church, during my 2000 trip to Northern Ireland. The two sites are only about a mile from each other. Templastragh dates to the beginnings of Christian Ireland and was linked with the O'Kane family in the late 1500s and 1600s. I have been there several times and it is a haunting and ancient place. It is mostly ruins now, only the walls remain and rubble of stone here and there. In the church and around it are a dozen or so burial stones including the large McCain stone. The Ordnance Survey Memoirs of the 1830s say it is the "Irish" cemetery by which they meant a Catholic cemetery. The Protestant cemetery of that area was a hundred or so yards north of the church ruins. The McCain burial stone is inside the walls of Templastragh Church in the Irish cemetery. Did this mean we had some deep connection to this old O'Kane location? I wondered why the Bushmills' McCains who were buried there would use the Irish Catholic Church yard in Templastragh. All of Joe McKane's people were Presbyterians, but I also knew that some of the O'Kane family from that area had converted to the Presbyterian faith in the

1700s. Did our McCains being buried in an O'Kane historical building mean that we had a connection to them? That was the question.

Templastragh Church itself is not large. As my friend Austin Rock put it, you would barely have room to swing a dead cat around in it. The church figures prominently in many old Irish stories and legends. It is part of the fabric of Irish history, which is saying a lot. I was impressed that members of our family are buried in the middle of the Templastragh Church. The church is located near Portbraddon on a cliff top. It is hard to say with complete certainty how old it is, the present building dates to the medieval times, but a church has stood on the site since the sixth century. In the ruins of the church today, on the northwest end, is an early form of a Celtic cross, which is believed to have been part of the original structure. It is a remarkable piece of early Irish stonework. The church is sitting in a farmer's field today, but it is well worth stopping the car and getting a little mud on your boots. Just remember to shut any gates you open going through the fields. In 1830, a British survey team wrote this note about Templastragh.

> The graveyard is small and enclosed partly by the church walls and partly by a stone and clay ditch. The number of headstones are very limited. The following are amongst the Christian names and surnames on these headstones: male names, John, James, Laurence, William; female names, Chatrine, Margaret, Jean; surnames, Morrison, Halliday, Holliwoods, McCain, McLeese. The oldest

stone is 1790 and the greatest age on any of them 70 years. The old church and graveyard, described on the last 2 pages of Fair Sheets, are locally called the Irish Kirkyard, so called in consequence of being occupied chiefly by the Roman Catholic burials.[16]

In researching Templastragh, I found the works of north Antrim historian Robert McCahan. He was born in Ballycastle, County Antrim in 1863 and in his life he became an acknowledged expert on north Antrim history. In the late 1800s and early 1900s, he wrote a series of historical essays on locations in north Antrim, including the Templastragh. His own family was Presbyterian, but native Irish, a curious mix you find more frequently than books lead you to expect. Robert McCahan said of Templastragh, "It is apparently of great age, and may have marked the burying-place of the O'Cahans in the older graveyard..."[17] Robert McCahan was himself a descendant of the O'Kane family of Dunseverick and his surname, McCahan, is an anglicized form of Mac Catháin, the form of their surname used by his branch of the family.

For my research I needed a dozen or so O'Kane men to do the DNA test. O'Kane is anglicized as Cain, Kane, Cahan, Kean, with and without a Mac or O prefix. It was a plausible origin of our McCain family, especially given the fact that members of our family are buried in the middle of

---

[16] Angélique Day, ed., Patrick McWilliams, ed., and Nóirín Dobson, ed., *Ordance Survey Memoirs of Ireland*, vol.24. (Belfast: The Institute of Irish Studies, The Queen's University of Belfast, 1994), 18.
[17] Robert McCahan, *M'Cahan's Local Histories* (Coleraine: Glens of Antrim Historical Society, 1988), 20.

Templastragh Church. So in the autumn of 2004 I returned to Ulster to enlist as many O'Kane men as I could to participate in the DNA project.

The trip in 2004 was special on several accounts. My oldest son, Donovan, accompanied me. Donovan is a professional musician, a very good one. He played his first paying gig at age 11. He grew up on stage, playing hundreds of festivals, live radio shows, and TV programs. He has worked with Bobby Whitlock of Derek and the Dominoes, and been on stage with the Oak Ridge Boys, Marty Stuart, and the Del McCoury band. I arranged for a small tour for him on the 2004 trip and I played rhythm guitar accompaniment. Some of the highlights were performances on the *Sin É* program in Dublin, on Tommy Sands' *County Céilí* Program in Belfast, and traditional music venues such as Mary McBride's Bar in Cushendun in the Antrim Glens, and Sandino's Pub in Derry. To be in Ireland or Northern Ireland is always fun, but to be there playing music raises the level of fun considerably.

During this trip, we stayed in Dungiven, the epicenter of the O'Kane clan in Ireland. The *craic* was good there. We stayed with Kevin O'Kane and the whole O'Kane clan treated us like royalty. We dined on salmon from the River Roe and there was not a night that we did not have music and drink. We enjoyed a lovely afternoon one day with Seamus O'Kane at his house just outside Dungiven. Seamus is *the* master bodhrán maker in Ireland and first level player. When we went to his house, we only had a couple of hours to visit because Seamus, Donovan and I, all had to play gigs that night. It was an enjoyable couple of hours, however. Seamus served us tea and farmbrack. Then he produced his bodhrán and Donovan took his mandolin out. They played harp tune after harp together. Both of them love Irish harp music and Don had, over the years, learned quite a repertoire. One of the greatest Irish harpist and composers was Ruairi Dall O'Kane (circa 1570 -1650) and his music is of stunning beauty. After the collapse of the Gaelic order and the Flight of the Earls in 1607, Ruairi made his way to Edinburgh, Scotland and there became one of the most famous musicians of his day. He wrote what most people call *Danny Boy*. The real name of the song is *Aisling an Óg Fhír* (dream of the young man). I also played a few songs with Donovan and Seamus that day and it was one of the most memorable moments of my 2004 trip.

One of the sons of Seamus O'Kane, Murrough, is also a world class musician on flute and whistle. We had an opportunity to play together casually at an O'Kane party, one that lasted literally all night. Murrough sat in with us when we played at Sandino's Pub in Derry. Murrough was a member of the legendary Ulster group *Óige*, a traditional band in the 1990s. We also got to play with Seán Quinn, a virtuoso piano accordion player and owner of Glens Music studio in Cushendun, County Antrim. Donovan and I, one blurry eyed Sunday morning after a gig, put down some tracks in Glens Music studio and a few of them you can hear on my son's first album, *Traveller's Way*.

Seán Quinn was good enough to sit in with us when we played Mary McBride's bar. McBride's is a great place to have real Irish seafood, ale, and listen to traditional music. I witnessed my son's stage craft that night. As we were playing, some brawny biker dudes came in. One had on a black T-shirt with bold white lettering which read, "Fuck The World." My son was at the mic and without hesitation greeted the man with, "I guess we know your foreign policy." The man laughed as did the entire room and the music resumed.

There is always magic in Ireland. One day on this trip, Donovan and I had no where we had to be, so we took a long drive into the Sperrins Mountains south of Dungiven to see the Aughlish Stone Circles. They are not easy to find as they are way up in the mountains and down several one lane roads, none of which are marked. After making several unproductive laps on beautiful mountain roads Donovan and I decided to ask for directions. We saw a man working in his front garden and I stopped the car. Donovan got out to ask him if he knew how to get to the Aughlish Stone Circles. As fate would have it (but this sort of thing is so typical in Ireland), the man looked up and greeted both Donovan and me by our first names. It was Liam, an accordion player with whom we had sat in with the night before at Arcade Bar in Dungiven. Liam told us to visit Ivar Canning and gave us directions to his house.

Ivar is a large holding farmer who lived up in the mountains. We proceeded up a winding road, through fields and woods, until we found the long driveway that led to Ivar's house. We pulled up to his house which was surrounded by a collection of barns and out buildings typical of a working farm and knocked on his door. Five minutes later, we were having tea and farmbrack in Ivar's warm and cozy kitchen while he told us about the standings stones of Aughlish, which were on his land. There is more to Ivar than a simple sheep farmer. He is highly intelligent and studies ancient sites around the world, an endeavor started by his fascination with the Aughlish stones on his own land. He explained to Donovan and me an interesting and complex theory of how they were related and, in a point I did not quite get, somehow connected to the Old Testament. As part of his interest and studies, he has journeyed to the Pyramids, Machu Picchu, Angkor Wat, and many other ancient sites, but none older than his own Aughlish standings stones. He packed Donovan and me into an old model of Land Rover and we proceeded down a road, more of a path really, and then left the road to go overland to the stones. It was an incredible place; mystical, beautiful, stunning. Ivar walked us over the site explaining various aspects of the layout of the stones. The site features a group of circles including one with 41 small stones and a fallen stone of almost five feet high at the south end, with another of the same height outside the circle to the north. There are three other circles, or parts of circles, with alignments, one of which stretches for 60 feet. The stone circles function as solar and lunar calendars. Like Stonehenge, Aughlish dates to Neolithic times, over 5000 years ago.

Toward the end of our Irish adventure, I took Donovan to the village of An Cheathrú Rua in Connemara and out to Inis Mór in the Aran Islands. It was a beautiful bright sunny day when we visited Inis Mór. We bicycled from Cill Rónáin to Dun Aonghasa, the magnificent second-century BC Celtic fort on the west side of the island. This was a bicycle ride that nearly killed me, but was a sublime experience for my 17 year old son. He used a photo taken at Dun Aonghasa that day for the cover of his album.

In between music and our rambles, I managed to interest a good dozen O'Kane families in participating in the McCain DNA Project. I would find out if their ancestors were the origins of our McCains. In early 2005, the O'Kane families' DNA results started coming in. I was impressed with their results because they all were related to each other. One O'Kane man found out his wife, whose maiden name was also O'Kane, was his cousin, albeit distant. This was discovered when his wife's brother did the test. These O'Kane families really are a bona fide old Irish clan. Some of their DNA matches went to a common ancestor that lived several generations ago and others to an ancestor that lived hundreds of years ago, but they all shared the same paternal line that went back to that one early medieval male ancestor. However, they were not related to the McCains and our family did not have O'Kane origins. I was slightly disappointed as their family, their clan, is a great one.

Despite this minor let down, the DNA Project was successful beyond my grandest hopes. The most important goal of finding the McCains in Ireland was achieved. The DNA matches also revealed a shift in the geography of the family. I had assumed we were from County Antrim, but as more McCain DNA matches came in, it became clear that the *home* county of the family was Donegal and the Antrim McCains were an offshoot of the Donegal McCains. We were all paternally related, all descendants of the same McCain patriarch, but I had not yet discovered this patriarch.

By 2008, more Irish and Northern Irish McCains had been located and I wanted to visit them. Fate stepped in to make this trip possible when the Ulster American Folk Park invited me to present a paper on the use of DNA in Ulster family history research. Jim McKane and I had started another DNA Project called the Ulster Heritage DNA Project in 2007.

We wanted to help other families in the Diaspora find their kinfolk in Ulster. So I went to the Ulster American Folk Park in the summer of 2008 to present the work being done by the Ulster Heritage Project. It was an interesting year to be a McCain due to John McCain's run for the presidency. Even his distant cousins were asked for interviews I found out. The best part of this trip was I would get to meet many McCain families in Donegal and Tyrone that I knew were my family.

The Finn Valley

In 2008, the Seventeenth Ulster American Heritage Symposium was held at the Ulster American Folk Park in County Tyrone. I was there to present a paper on the Ulster Heritage DNA Project. The symposium has met every two years since 1976 and alternates between co-sponsoring universities, museums, and historical societies, in Ulster and the United States. I presented a paper on the McCain Family DNA Project at the sixteenth symposium held in Knoxville, Tennessee. The stated theme of the seventeenth symposium was the *Changing Perspectives 1607-2007*. This was fitting as I had decided several years ago that the Ulster Scots and their offshoot, the Scots-Irish, needed re-examination. There is a shallow Ulster Scots stereotype constructed in late Victorian times and it obscures a more complex history that needs to be told. This is not a case of revisionism, but rather the need to add more details and facts to the story. My trip had a dual purpose. After the symposium I arranged to visit with many of my McCain kinsfolk in Donegal.

The Ulster American Folk Park is located just north of Omagh. I took the bus from Dublin airport to Omagh early on a summer's morning in late June. Bus Éireann is an enjoyable way to see Ireland and I often travelled by bus on my stays there. Omagh is known for the infamous bombing which took place on 15 August 1998. The bombing was done by a group called the *Real Irish Republican Army*, which in turn was a splinter group from the Provisional Irish Republican Army, better known as the IRA. On that day, 29 people were killed by the explosion and another 220 were injured. There were Catholics and Protestants among the victims, as well as several tourists from the Republic of Ireland and Spain. To say the bombing was pointless and a tragedy is the definition of an understatement. The bombing, understandably, created an international outcry against the RIRA and did much to give the Northern Ireland peace process a needed boost.

The Ulster American Folk Park was established in 1976 and was Northern Ireland's contribution to the American bicentenary. The park is built around the homestead of Thomas Mellon who in 1818 at age 5 immigrated with his family to western Pennsylvania. Thomas Mellon became wealthy and he eventually returned to Ireland to visit the home of his birth. One of his descendants, Matthew Mellon, organized the restoration of the Mellon home in County Tyrone. In the 1970s, Matthew Mellon was the force behind the creation of the Ulster American Folk Park, with the Mellon home as a primary exhibit. Since its opening in July 1976, the park has grown rapidly with the addition of several historical exhibit buildings and a research center. The museum now represents a broad spectrum of the history of eighteenth and nineteenth-century emigration from Ulster to America.

Brian Lambkin is the Director of the Centre for Migration Studies at the Ulster American Folk Park, which organized the symposium. Brian is a talented writer with several well received books on the history of Ulster migration. On my first day at the Folk Park, we were treated to a bus tour of various sights, mostly in the Lagan district in east Donegal, which is McCain country. While bouncing along on the country roads I heard historian Peter Gilmore, sitting behind me on the bus, speaking Irish to a man seated beside him. With my Mississippi Irish, I joined in the conversation and Brian Lambkin, seated nearby, also joined in the conversation, in Irish. It struck me as interesting that two Americans of Scots-Irish ancestry were on a bus speaking in Irish with the Director of the Centre for Migration Studies, but it is also suggestive of the complex history of the Ulster Scots.

I found Omagh to be more postmodern urban British than Irish. I have been visiting Ireland since the mid-1970s and have spent more time in Connemara than any other part of the country. For this reason my idea of Ireland is colored by a very Gaelic lens. I judge Irishness by how close it is to Connemara standards. Most of the inhabitants of what used to be the Celtic Tiger would laugh at my notions. Then again there are people in Ireland that know exactly what I'm talking about. Everywhere I went in Omagh I heard British top 40 pop music. I thought that the US and Allied troops in Afghanistan and Iraq should have used these sounds to extract information from captured enemy combatants. Forget water-boarding, this is much worse. My opinion of Omagh is unfair really, as I was only there for a few days, but I did get the impression that all the better aspects of Northern Irish society and culture were being jettisoned as fast as possible and replaced by a lager drinking, fast food eating, disposable pop culture, which gave me the heebie-jeebies. If I had more time, I would have sought out the traditional music scene there. Traditional musicians could have shown me a different and better Omagh. One day, I shall go back and do just that.

The symposium was well run and interesting. Some of the speakers and papers that stand out to me are Peter Gilmore, *When Pittsburgh's 'Scotch-Irish' were 'Irish'*; Michael Montgomery, *An Appalachian Mist Has Descended upon Ulster*; Nini Rodgers, *Ramelton in the Caribbean: Presbyterians and the plantation complex, 1730 – 1857*; and Peter M. Toner, *Confusing Identities: The Gaeltachtaí in New Brunswick, 1901*. These are just a few among many excellent papers presented and they give an idea of the focus of the current research in Ulster heritage.

Omagh is a great place to learn Polish and listen to British pop music, but after the symposium I was on to the Finn Valley in Donegal and visits with my McCains. My hosts in the Finn Valley were the larger than life figure of Ivan Knox and his beautiful wife Letitia. Ivan Knox's mother was Sarah McKane making Ivan a distant cousin of mine. Even distant cousins are family in Ireland and Mississippi. The Finn Valley is a beautiful scenic area and home to a people that are descendants of local Irish clans and Ulster Scots. The valley starts up near Baile Na Finne and runs generally east through An Clóchan, down to the twin towns of Ballybofey and Stranorlar, then on to Castlefinn and on further to Lifford on the Foyle River. I stayed at the Knox's home in Corcam which is a mile east of Stranorlar. From there Ivan showed me around and introduced me to many of the McCain families in east Donegal and northwest Tyrone. Ivan is a walking library of information about many families in the district and is easily the most knowledgeable man around concerning the Donegal McCains.

When I met Ivan in person, he reminded me of the actor Victor McLaglen. Victor McLaglen played the part of Red Will Danaher in *The Quiet Man*, as aficionados of that famous John Wayne film know. Ivan is much more intellectual than Will Danaher was and I suspect Ivan Knox could have given both the Danaher and Seán Thorton a run for their money if it came down to fists. Ivan is dominant in his milieu, the way Red Will Danaher was in Inisfree. Ivan is also a renaissance man. He is a self-made businessman, a farmer, and in retirement he has become an excellent historian, writer, and poet. His interests include the lore and folkways of the Finn Valley. He is a published poet and tradition keeper. He wrote *50 Original Picture Poems of People and Places Around the Finn Valley* in 2003 and is credited by the Irish government as being a leader in the revival of the Irish Mummer tradition in Ulster. He is one of the movers and shakers in the Finn Valley. He was a friend of the Canadian business baron, Wallace McCain of the New Brunswick McCains, who passed away in the spring of 2011. Many of the McCains in the Diaspora that return to Ireland for a visit find themselves sitting in a chair beside Ivan Knox with a restorative drink.

Ivan grew up on the family farm at Labadoo, not far from Stranorlar, in the Finn Valley. He made his first business purchase at age 12, a donkey he bought for 3 Irish punts. Ivan and his mother, Sarah Knox née McKane, began a poultry business in the late 1950s. On 5 September 1958, Ivan sold the family's first chickens to Mrs. Harry Kee, of the famous Kee's Hotel in Stranorlar, for two shillings and 6 pence per pound, killed, plucked and delivered. That was the beginning of *Finn View Poultry Products Ltd.* Ivan ran the firm for years and now has handed its day to day operations over to his sons. They still supply high quality poultry and other products to the leading restaurants and hotels in the region. Kee's Hotel is still there, a charming Irish hotel with an excellent restaurant and pub.

Ivan Knox comes from Ulster Scot Planter stock, but his roots are now in the brown fertile soil of the Finn Valley. In the Finn Valley the Ulster Scots presence is strong and Lallans is still spoken. Ivan and Letitia are active in the Presbyterian Church in Stranorlar and are often seen on the streets and roads around the district. The Knox family is a part of Ireland that is fast fading, unfortunately. They represent all the better aspects of the Ulster Scot community. They are honest, hardworking, Church going folk, quick with a smile, and with a wry sense of humor that makes them enjoyable to be around, and your glass will not go dry in their company.

There are parties in Ulster that like to make the most of the differences between the Ulster Scot and the native Irish Gael. There are differences of course, but there are also similarities and a shared inheritance as well. Knox is also a Gaelic origin surname, a topographical origin name from *Cnoc*, meaning "hill." Ivan is a participant in the Ulster Heritage DNA Project and his genetic roots are indigenous Atlantic Zone Celt which is dominant in both Ireland and Scotland. After I returned back to Mississippi, I helped the Knox family with their DNA test analysis. Ivan's test results matched a dozen Knox families in the southern USA from Alabama, Mississippi, Arkansas, and Texas, more cousins for Ivan. The legacy of Ulster in North America comes from its many sons and daughters that immigrated here and this legacy is large indeed.

The week I spent with Ivan and Letitia was a whirlwind; a blitzkrieg of visits to McCain families and their in-laws. It was a week of good restaurants, hearth sides with glasses of whiskey in our hands, quiet pubs, rain, narrow single lane roads, and fun. I would list every family I visited if I could, I did take notes, but often I had no time to properly record events. There were the Drumboe McKanes, the Whitehill McKanes with Wesley's broken foot, the St Johnston McKeans, Ian and Joyce McKean of Port Hall and their impressive house (which I hope to visit again), then on to McKanes across the Foyle in Tyrone, and related families such as the Knoxes, Wilsons and Pattersons. Their kindness and hospitality was overwhelming. It was a busy and enjoyable week punctuated with good food and drink.

One day we had supper at *Dom's Pier One* in Donegal Town. Dom's has some of the best roast lamb in the world. While we were there, Ivan spotted the Irish An Tániste (vice Prime Minister), Mary Coughlan, and he took her by the hand and led her to our table where we enjoyed a lively introduction and conversation. I asked her if Senator McCain could count on her support during the upcoming presidential election. She smiled and, with a wink, explained these were deep matters and the Irish government does not, as a rule, intervene in the American elections. Mary Coughlan is an intelligent, easy going woman and it was a pleasure meeting her. She served as a Teachta Dála (representative) for Donegal South West constituency from 1987-2011. Like many other Irish politicians, Mary lost her re-election bid in 2011, a casualty of the political turmoil produced by the collapse of the Celtic Tiger. At the end of my visit, Ivan and Letitia took me to their beach home in Rossnowlagh in southwest Donegal, where we stayed for a couple of days. There I saw epic sunsets and listened to the Atlantic as it rolls in upon the strand. There is a cozy pub on the hillside above the beach, called the *Smuggler's Creek,* where I sat with family and friends and enjoyed a Guinness or three as we looked down upon the beach and to the Atlantic beyond. The quality of such an experience is beyond words.

I took an immediate liking to the Finn Valley. It is not often on the tourist maps, but it has a lot of quality. Stranorlar and Ballybofey are twin towns separated by the Finn river. Both Gaelic and Lallans were spoken in Stranorlar for a long time, though now English is the dominant language. Some of the early Presbyterian Ulster Scots in Stranorlar were Gaelic speaking but, gradually over time, Lallans became more common. By the 1700s, many of the Gaelic speakers in the rural area west of Stranorlar used Lallans as a second language, rather than English. This was because they would take seasonal employment among the Ulster Scots in and around Stranorlar. This rich language environment has not gone unnoticed. In 2010 the Fiach Art Circle published *Treasure Each Voice, 400 years of Anglo-Irish, Irish and Ulster-Scots Literature From Stranorlar.* The book includes prose and verse in English, Gaelic, and Lallans. It is a celebration and history of the three languages of Stranorlar. I wrote a chapter in the book, in Gaelic, *Mo Shinsir Gaeil* (My Gaelic Ancestry).

In 2008, I wrote a group of articles for the Irish newspaper *The Finn Valley Voice*. The paper is based in Stranorlar and its editor is Celine McGlynn. It is an old fashioned regional paper that was founded in 1994 and it is one of the two oldest independent newspapers that have survived in Ireland, the other one being the *Tirconaill Tribune*. It is unique in another regard in that it is owned by an all lady group. Celine not only edits and manages the newspaper, but she is also an accomplished artist. Celine does oil paintings of Donegal landscapes and her works have appeared in the Screig Gallery, in Fintown. Celine wanted to run some articles to highlight the growing interest in John McCain's presidential bid. I suggested to Celine a column for her paper which would address the McCain connection to the district and other topics of interest. I suggested we call the column *McCain's Corner*. Celine McGlynn thought my *McCain's Corner* idea a good one and, in the spring of 2008, I began a series of articles that appeared as the *McKane's Corner* column in the Finn Valley Voice.

When I suggested that name, I did not know that there exists a landmark called *McKane's Corner*. In the late 1800s, John McKane of Trenamullin founded *McKane's General Merchants Shop* at the corner of Chapel Street and Main Street in Stranorlar. From the early 1900s this street corner was used by the local men to meet together and talk about the issues of the day and to enjoy the craic. It became known as McKane's Corner and remains to this day a Stranorlar landmark. Pat Holland, a reporter with the *Finn Valley Voice*, told me of a poignant letter he read about McKane's Corner. The letter was written in 1917 by Patrick Kelly, who was away fighting in World War I. He sent a letter home to his family and toward the end he wrote, "tell me how they are getting on about McKane's Corner, you can tell them all I was asking for them." Poor Patrick was killed shortly after posting the letter home. The letter is still in existence, kept by his grandnephew, Jonathan Kelly.

Pat gave me a tour around the twin towns and took me to McKane's Corner. On the day we stopped at the corner, there were several older gentlemen seated there, deep in conversation. They were keeping up the McKane's Corner tradition of meeting to chat about the events of the day. We talked to them and took photographs. They were delighted, as were we. Pat and I also solved a mystery while we were at McKane's Corner. The location of the original sign of McKane's General Merchants Shop was unknown. Many feared it had been taken down and was rotting away in some barn, or worse, had been burned as trash. But we found it that day. *The Flower Shop* is now in the building that once was McKane's General Merchants and as we were looking at the current florist's sign we noticed that behind it was the original McKane's sign. It is worth stopping the car to take a few photos on McKane's Corner, and besides, Kee's Hotel and bar are just a few steps away.

Pat Holland also took me to the Jackson's Hotel in Ballybofey. There I heard the real story behind Irish Coffee, which is worth repeating. There is a common and widely held myth that Irish Coffee, that wonderful concoction, was first created in the bar in Shannon Airport. It is true this drink was served there at an early date, but it was not the first place to serve it. Irish Coffee originated in County Donegal at Jackson's Hotel in Ballybofey.

There was a seaman named Joe Jackson, a Derry man, who served in the Merchant Navy during World War II. It was his misfortune to be on a ship that was torpedoed in the north Atlantic. When he was rescued, he was suffering from exposure and was revived with a high proof drink made from coffee and rum, which was a British Navy practice of the day. The rest of Joe Jackson's service was in the eastern Mediterranean and there he was exposed to drinks containing cream, sugar, and spirits. When the war was over, Joe returned home to Ireland and married a woman in the catering business in Ballybofey. Joe purchased a hotel in Ballybofey in the late 1940s and, calling upon his experiences during the war, began to experiment with new drinks. One of his creations was *Irish Coffee* and it became a specialty of the house. This is the familiar drink made of strong black coffee, sugar, Irish whiskey, and a layer of slightly thickened cream on top. In the early 1950s, a Scottish motoring magazine published an account of Joe Jackson's Irish Coffee and from this humble start the popularity of the drink grew in the outside world. The drink was replicated, according to lore, on 10 November 1952 in the bar of Shannon airport. But this was several years after Jackson's Hotel began serving the drink. Perhaps it was a public relations coup or perhaps Donegal was in those days too distant and remote for news to travel, but for whatever reason, the Shannon airport origin myth for Irish Coffee began to take root. To drink an Irish Coffee in the establishment where it was invented, however, one must go to Jackson's Hotel, Ballybofey, Donegal, Ireland.

Pat Holland also was kind enough to handle some of the media requests for interviews with me. Because of Senator John McCain's presidential run, there was interest in even a cousin of his on a ramble in Donegal. I did several radio interviews, one on the *Shaun Doherty Show* on Highland Radio in Letterkenny. I had the distinct impression that ole Shaun thought any supporter or worse a kinsman of Senator John McCain was akin to the devil himself, but that sort of ignorance of American politics is common within the Irish media. The most fascinating aspect of the interview was meeting an American in the waiting room prior to going on air. He was a man from Arizona, of Donegal ancestry. He was there visiting family as I was. In whispered voice he told me that if I had any investments I had better liquidate them as soon as I got back. Now, this was the first week of July 2008, before any media knowledge of the coming collapse of the stock markets and the real estate bubble. Those events were to come to a head in the ensuing months during the last weeks of the election campaign. The gentleman from Arizona, however, knew about it and told me it was all a conspiracy. It was one of those interesting things that happen to you on the road. None the less, sitting here six years later, it amazes me how much he knew about the future economic collapse.

I returned home to Mississippi pleased. I had met a small army of McCain kinsfolk and numerous in-laws of our family. I had seen old McCain homesteads and I had absorbed a lot of Donegal culture. However, I had not learned any more about the origins of the McCains. This was about to change. In the fall of 2008, the McCain DNA Project turned up new DNA matches of great interest. These matches were all from mid-Argyll, in the Highlands of Scotland. This was the beginning of unraveling the mystery of the McCains' origins.

The author's grandfather, Leslie Harris McCain (on right),
picking cotton with his family, circa 1910, Vaiden, Mississippi

Author, Elizabeth Spencer of the Teoc McCains

Senator John McCain with Irish Taoiseach, Bertie Ahern

Joe McKane of Ballywatt, County Antrim

Ivar Canning and Donovan McCain at the Aughlish stone circles

Seamus O'Kane and Donovan McCain
enjoying a musical session together

McKane's General Merchants (now the Flower Shop),
McKane's Corner, Stranorlar

Local lads deliberating on the news of the day at McKane's Corner

The burial stone of Donnchadh Rua Mac Ailein,
known in history as Duncan McCain

Dr. Joseph McKane (on left) of Glasgow
with Jim McKane of Wiarton, Ontario
beside the Donnchadh Rua Mac Ailein stone

Ian McKean (on left) in front of his residence at Porthall
with Ivan Knox of Finn Valley

The house of Ian and Joyce McKean at Porthall on the Foyle River

An early McCain dwelling in the Finn Valley, circa early 1700s
now converted to a barn

The Finn Valley

Mongavlin castle, residence of Iníon Dubh
and where the McCains first appear in Ireland

Argyll

I had found the McCains that remained in Ireland, exactly what I wanted to accomplish when I began my odyssey so many years ago. I could have stopped there and been content, but now I wanted to discover our origins or even the progenitor of the family. Among the McCains I visited in Ireland, there was a general sense of being from Scotland, but none of them had specific knowledge or details. Ironically, the McCains in New England and in Mississippi were the only branches of the family that had oral history that remembered us being Highland Scots and having links to Argyll. When new DNA matches appeared in the fall of 2008 showing a definite connection to mid-Argyll, I felt like it was possible to finally discover our origins.

The Y chromosome data base was then and is today growing fast for several reasons, ancestor worship among them. There is a great interest in genetic genealogy and family history in the Irish and Scottish Diaspora and I know why. Irish and Scots put great value on blood, kinship, family relations, and ancestors. Perhaps it is the nature of a Diaspora to search for identity and tribal connections. The Irish and Scots have a history of migration to distant lands and were hard pressed to retain their identity and language. DNA testing reconnects these families with their clan, tribe, and their past. This worked to my advantage because the descendants of the Irish and Scots have turned to DNA testing in disproportionately large numbers compared to other ethnic groups.

As the Y chromosome data base grew, the McCains collected more matches to a paternal kinship group in mid Argyll. I began going through the pre 1600 records of the area hunting for signs of the McCains. While doing this I discovered that the McCain surname itself carries an important clue about our Argyll origins. McCains are no different than millions of Gaelic families in the Diaspora in that most of our surnames have been changed from the native Gaelic into an English language form. With Gaels, knowing the original Gaelic form of a surname is a good starting point when beginning the task of finding ancestors. The McCain surname is linked to Argyll through its etymology.

You would think the etymology of the surname McCain would be simple enough, but it is not. If you open a standard Irish or Scottish surname book, it normally says *McCain is the anglicized form of the Scottish name Mac Iain.* This is usually followed by a reference to either the Glencoe or Ardnamurchan *Mac Iain* families of Scotland. What these books do not tell you is there were several dozen McCain families scattered throughout the Gaelic speaking world. To complicate matters, there are several Gaelic surnames that have been anglicized as McCain. A list would include the surnames *Mac Eáin, Mac Catháin, Mac Aodháin, Mac Caodháin,* and *Ó Catháin.* Notice the surname book version, *Mac Iain,* is not listed. This is because *Iain* and *Mac Iain* are late entries into the Gaelic world. *Iain* is a relatively modern Scottish Gaelic name and it is not found in old records. Fortunately, in Donegal and in mid Argyll there is only one surname anglicized as McCain, which is *Mac Eáin*.

Eáin (said Ane) is a variation of the common Gaelic name *Eóin* (said Owen). The *Eáin* form is peculiar to Argyll and the southern Hebrides and it is considered Scottish Gaelic in origin. The surname was introduced into Donegal by Argyll Gaels that settled there in the 1500s. *Eóin* appears in early medieval Irish sources and is the Gaelic form of the Latin name *Iohannes*, or as English speakers know the name, *John*. *Iohannes* is itself a loan word to Latin from the Hebrew *Yohanan* (in full *y'hohanan*) meaning "Jehovah has favored." Senator John McCain has the name *Iohannes* twice in his name, an English form for his given name and a Gaelic form in his surname. My older son's name, including his confirmation saint's name, is John William Seán Donovan McCain, which has three forms of *Iohannes* in his name! Seán came into Gaelic from the French form of the Latin *Iohannes* which was *Jehan* and Gaelicized as *Seán*. The Gaelic names *Seán*, *Eóin*, and *Eáin*, all come from the Latin *Iohannes*.

As you read through the Gaelic manuscripts you will not find any evidence of the variant *Eáin* form of *Eóin* until 1499 AD. That year in the *Annals of Connacht* one writer spelled the name of *Eóin Mór Mac Dónaill*, King of the Isles, as *Eighín Mor Mac Domnaill*, with *Eighín* being a slender vowel form of *Eáin*. This Eóin Mór Mac Dónaill was the chief of the McDonalds in Argyll, Islay and north Antrim. From that time on you can find the name sporadically written to reflect this *Eáin* form, but *Eóin* was still the dominant written form in literary Irish regardless if the name was said *Eóin* or *Eáin*. Literary Irish was the Gaelic used in both Ireland and Scotland by the educated classes.

By the mid-1600s, the *Mac Eáin* variation had its own spelling in literary Irish. The Scottish Mac Mhuirich family of Islay, historians and tradition keepers for the McDonalds, used several similar spellings of the surname when writing in the mid-1600s. In their *Red Book of Clanranald,* they spelled the surname *mac Ceaain, Mac Eaain* and *Mac Ea'ain.* The *mac Ceaain* spelling is an abbreviated form of the longer *Mac Mhic Eaain,* a clan surname form meaning "son of (the) son of Eáin." This form functions much like the Ó does in Gaelic surnames, especially Irish ones. I asked the Sabhal Mòr Ostaig, which is the Gaelic college on the Isle of Skye, for the current spelling in Scot's Gaelic and they gave me *Mac Eain,* with no accent over the "a." *Mac Eáin* is the modern Ulster Gaelic form.

The Lallans spellings also demonstrate the pronunciation shift from *Mac Eóin* to *Mac Eáin* by the 1500s in Argyll. Lallans spellings of *Mac Eáin* from that time were *McAne, McEan, Makayn, Mcayne, McEan,* and *McKean.* In my research, I made an interesting discovery. In the 1400s, the northern Spanish and Portuguese form of the Latin *Iohannes* was *Ean.* In the northwest Spanish dialects and Portuguese the surname form of *Ean* was *Eanes* and *Eannes.* The *es* suffix functions like the Gaelic *Mac.* So *Eannes* means *Son of Iohannes* as does *Mac Eáin.* In modern Spanish, you see this surname written Yanes and Yáñes. It did occur to me there might have been some connection there, perhaps a loan word that had come into use from Portuguese or Spanish to Gaelic due to the increasing contact between Argyll and Spain during that time, but it would be a difficult point to research.

The Gaelic etymology of our name pointed to Argyll and now there was a DNA link there as well. Additionally, I had the New England McKeens' oral history of an ancestor known as William McKean "the soldier" from Argyll and the Teoc Mississippi McCains oral history in which we were also Highland Gaels who were supporters of Mary Queen of Scots. As the McCain DNA Project progressed from 2008 to 2013, both of these oral histories gained considerable support. Working with DNA on a point of deep ancestry is like trolling a fishing line. You put your bait on and make your run, you don't know when or where, but you hope and even expect something to hit the line eventually and that is what happened. Some of the new McCain DNA matches had specific locations with names of villages and settlements. These were in the parish of Kilmichael Glassary in mid Argyll. I now had a specific place to hunt for McCains.

The first DNA match in mid Argyll was to a family from Lochgilphead, a small town in Kilmichael Glassary parish. This match made a piece of information that had been sent to me years before suddenly relevant. I had learned about a McCain family that lived near Lochgilphead through serendipity. A good friend, Raymond McQuilkin of Knoxville, Tennessee, was also hunting for his Argyll ancestors. In his search, he discovered an interesting McCain reference and mailed me a copy. It was a line drawing of a burial stone slab and notes done by Captain T. P. White that had been published in 1875 in his *Archaeological Sketches in Scotland: Knapdale and Gigha.* The drawing and notes of Captain White concerned a man he called Duncan M'Cane who had a burial stone slab in Kilmichael Glassary village, which is only four miles northwest of Lochgilphead. I had received this information in the late 1990s and filed it away as an interesting piece of lore, but I had no reason to believe it was linked to our family. Captain White was drawn to a magnificent example of late medieval Gaelic art, the stone slab dedicated to Duncan McCane. Here are Captain White's notes on the slab:

> we have a very large and fine slab of a type seen only, so far as I am yet aware, at Kilmichael-Glassary, near Lochgilphead. The arrangement of the stems and foliage, and the peculiar shape of the latter with the small round buttons at their springing from the stem, are what give the specific character to this slab. The animals, also, are of an odd style, and somewhat stiff in their outlining. The inscription here is a fine specimen of the manner in which the lettering of the old ecclesiastical carvings was made to subserve the purposes of embellishment as well as those of a record. The writing in this case is tolerably perfect, and there is no difficulty in reading the initiator words, "Hic iacet Duncanus." Now, in 1479, King James III granted to Colin, Earl of Argyll, the lands of Gareald, Craigenewir (in the valley of the Add), and Tanglandles (within the barony of Glassary), resigned by Duncan Makcane. With the aid of this information, if

we turn again to the inscription, the following, I think, can be deciphered—

Hic iacet Duncanus Mor M'Cane

--and at the top of the slab the name "Lachlan." This appears to be one of those rare instances where we are enabled to identify a mediaeval tombstone in the West Highlands with a substantive individual of whom there is documentary record. The date of this slab may therefore be referred to about the close of the fifteenth century. The sword-hilt and guard figured on it are of a pattern we have seen once in Knapdale, and are very prettily worked out.[18]

The man that Captain White calls Duncan Mor M'Cane was the historical figure he identified and this was his burial stone. However, Captain White did not read the inscription correctly or else he chose to call this man by the name he is known by in history. The inscription literally reads, "Hic Iacit Duncanus Roy M'Allen." Roy, in medieval Scotland was the Latinized form of the Gaelic epithet "Rua," which means "Red." In 1881, the stone was the subject of another study by James Drummond, who took photographs and did a rubbing. Drummond correctly read the stone's inscription as "Duncanus 'oy M'Allen."[19] The R of Roy had been worn away or damaged and was missing by the late 1800s. The inscription

[18] Capt. Thomas P White, *Archaeological Sketches in Scotland: Knapdale and Gigha*, (London: Royal Collection, 1875), pl XLVII.
[19] James Drummond, *Sculptured Monuments in Iona & The West Highland*, (Edinburgh, Society of Antiquaries of Scotland, 1881), 32, 33, plate LXXIII.

on the stone is this Duncan's genealogy and his father's name was "Allen." Duncan's name in Gaelic was Donnchadh Rua Mac Ailein, but he was known as Duncan McCain. For our purposes, we shall call him Duncan Roy McCain and in Gaelic Donnchadh Rua Mac Eáin. The why and how he was known as McCain will be explained later, for the moment the important element was our McCain family was connected, by a DNA match, to where he lived and was buried.

The initial DNA match in Kilmichael Glassary was to Stan McDonald of Park Forrest, Illinois. His ancestor was Thomas Andrew McDonald, born 1817, Lochgilphead, Kilmchael Glassary Parish, just a few miles from where Duncan Roy McCain was buried. Thomas McDonald was a Catholic, which could not have been easy for him and his family in those days in mid-Argyll. The Reformation came early to that part of Argyll and the wars between the Catholic McDonalds and the largely Presbyterian Campbells in the 1640s made the area like the Middle East of today. There was no Catholic Church in the area from the mid-1600s through the 1800s, as all of them had been turned into Protestant churches. The eighth Earl of Argyll, Giolla Easpuig Caimbeul (1607 – 1661) was known as the Covenanting Earl and, despite changing sides and religions several times, did much to end the official Catholic presence in mid-Argyll. Not to be deterred, some of the conservative families remained steadfast in their Catholic faith, Stan's ancestor being one of these.

Kilmichael Glassary is the name of the parish and is also the name of a village in the parish. Kilmichael Glassary parish is bordered by Loch Awe in the north and by Dunadd in the south, on the west by Kilmartin parish and to the east by

Loch Fyne.[20] It is not a large district. From Dunadd to Loch Awe is about twelve miles and from Loch Fyne to Kilmartin parish is half that distance. Kilmichael Glassary village was an early Christian center associated with nearby Dunadd. Dunadd is famous for its cup and ring marked stones that date back to the early medieval kingdom of Dál Riada, which had its capital there. Dunadd is where Saint Columba crowned Aodhan Mac Gabhran as the first Christian king of Dál Riada circa 574 AD. In Argyll, this Aodhan is remembered for having a son named Artur who in local lore is remembered as being the historical King Arthur, an interesting theory which has picked up some support in recent years. Saint Columba was active in Argyll and many of the place names in this district reflect these Christian roots; Kilmory, Kilmichael, Kilmartin, Kilberry, and Kilneuir, to name a few. The Kil prefix in village names usually comes from the Gaelic word *Cill*, meaning *cell* or *church,* and each place is where the Gaels of the area gathered to worship and celebrate the presence of the Christ.

I suspected that the short distance between Duncan Roy McCain's burial slab and where our McDonald DNA match lived was more than a coincidence and I searched for records on the Kilmichael Glassary McCain family. I found them in the Scottish Crown records and in the Argyll records compiled by various prominent families from the area. A McCain family thrived in Kilmichael Glassary from the early 1400s into the 1600s. Duncan Roy McCain was a member of this family. Duncan's father's name was Ailean Mac Eáin Riabhach and his grandfather's name was Eáin Riabhach. *Riabhach* is a hair color nickname that means "brownish or tawny with streaks of

---

[20] See Mid-Argyll map on page 1.

123

other color." Ailean Mac Eáin Riabhach became the seneschal (head legal official) and taoiseach (chief) of Kilmichael Glassary in 1436. Duncan Roy McCain was one of four sons of Ailean Mac Eáin Riabhach.

I ask the reader to be patient with my switching back and forth between spellings of McCain. I will mention again that in this book McCain equals McCane, M'Ean, Mac Eáin, McKane, McKain, McKean, and McKeen. There is a trend with modern historians to spell historical Gaelic surnames in modern standard Irish. This gets around having to deal with the multiple anglicized forms of Gaelic surnames that plague both Irish and Scottish history. When dealing with the pre 1600 McCains, I will use the original Mac Eáin spelling.

With a historical figure like Duncan Roy McCain there is usually a genealogy from late medieval Gaelic manuscripts available. There are several elaborate ones that do trace the line of his father back to the ancient kings of Ireland. It is tempting to use these, but the truth is Gaels were much like the English, French, and Spanish when it came to constructing a genealogy in those days. In late medieval times, one would hire a historian, called a *seanchaí*, who made sure his patron had an illustrious past that, inevitably, would lead back to the high kings of ancient Ireland. Historians have warned us for many years that these colorful genealogies should not always be taken literally. In recent years, DNA testing has dramatically confirmed this. Not to be deterred by this, generations of Mac and Os have stood in front of clan society tents at Irish and Scottish festivals and have been given their entire genealogy handed to them back to Niall of the Nine Hostages and beyond to Adam in some cases.

I would need something pithier and more recent than a medieval genealogy to explore the connections between Ailean Mac Eáin, along with his son Duncan Roy, and my family. I would have to find Ailean Mac Eáin and his descendants in the day to day records of the district in the 1500s and produce some evidence that supported that these descendants were our McCain family. I believed this was possible using the McCain DNA matches to families from Kilmichael Glassary. If I could do this, I could construct a reasonable history of the McCains prior to their migration to Ireland.

Duncan Roy McCain

Near the top of the cosmic list of foolish things to do is to get into a war in Afghanistan and not too far behind is to write about Gaelic kinship groups in Argyll. However, using DNA results as a guide I attempt the latter. Even having DNA results to guide us, this will be a difficult chapter for the reader to navigate. The world of Gaelic onomastics of the fifteenth and sixteenth centuries is a complex topic even for Gaelic speaking historians. I will try to make it as painless as possible and this will be the only chapter where I pull out all stops. I have also divided this chapter into two parts. Part one will outline my findings for the average reader and part two will go into the primary sources. This gives the reader the option of skipping part two and proceeding to the next very interesting chapter.

There were McCain DNA matches to families from Kilmichael Glassary and nearby areas in mid Argyll. All these families are paternally related to the McCains. I designated these families, including the McCains, the Mid Argyll Kinship Group. Analysis of the DNA results dated the time of the shared paternal ancestor to circa 1500s for most of the families, while others in the group were more distant. My goal was to find the descendants of Duncan Roy McCain and confirm that some of them took the surname McCain. If I could accomplish this, then I could make a good case that his family was the origin of our McCains.

The Mid Argyll Kinship Group includes the surnames, listed in their anglicized forms and then in Gaelic, McAlpin (Mac Ailpín), McCain (Mac Eáin), McDonald (Mac Dónaill), Duncan (Mac Donnchaidh), Henry (Mac Eanruig), and MacLea (Mac an Leagha).[21] These are not *clan* surnames and they do not relate to historical clans from mid-Argyll. They are surnames created from Gaelic patronymic naming customs. Surnames were not fixed in Argyll until around the late 1500s into the 1600s. Even then the use of clan surnames was not universal and was a form often found only on legal documents written by government officials.[22] Clan surnames were used more by the oldest sons of landed families and these names functioned as a title as well as a name. The fact that the Mid Argyll Kinship families shared the same paternal kinship but were using at least six different surnames is not unusual. They do share some obvious connections, however. They are from mid-Argyll and several of the families have primary source records that placed their ancestors in Kilmichael Glassary parish on lands that had been in the family of Ailean Mac Eáin. A connection to a specific piece of land is extremely important in research on Gaelic families. Land stayed with a family for centuries and was passed down to blood kin.

---

[21] McCain Family DNA Project, http://mccaindna.ulsterheritage.com/.
[22] Michael Newton, *A Handbook of the Scottish Gaelic World*, (Dublin: Four Courts Press, 2000), 136-7.

To link the McCains to Ailean Mac Eáin and his son, Duncan Roy McCain, I needed to confirm connections between the lands of Ailean Mac Eáin, his descendants, and the families of the Mid Argyll Kinship Group. It was not sufficient to find men with the Mid Argyll Kinship surnames in Kilmichael Glassary. Given Gaelic patronymic customs, there are many families that carry the surnames in the Mid Argyll Kinship Group as part of their name. Gaelic surnames from this period often carried short genealogies in them based on the derbhfine. The derbhfine name contained four generations of the man's family back to his paternal great grandfather. The derbhfine gradually gave way to a three generation format called a gelfine. It would be possible to confirm kinship to Ailean Mac Eáin and his sons if I could find descendants using derbhfine and gelfine surname forms.

This naming practice was important in the Gaelic world because their society was one of caste and heredity. Gaelic society needed to know not only your name, but the names of your father, grandfather, and great grandfather. It provided the information needed to explain who a man was and the lands and rights of his family within his district and society. An example of Gaelic surnames from this time: a man named Dónall Mac Ailein had a son named Lachlan who took the name Lachlan Mac Dónaill Mhic Ailein. His surname is Mac Dónaill and the Mhic Ailein tells you who his grandfather was.

Initially, I had difficulty finding the descendants of Ailean Mac Eáin and his sons. I discovered the reason for this when reading through records compiled by Sir Ian Douglas Campbell. Sir Ian Douglas Campbell (1903 – 1973) was the eleventh Duke of Argyll. One of his many accomplishments was allowing the manuscripts of his clan to be organized, cataloged, and transcripts produced. It was researchers from The Church of Jesus Christ of Latter-day Saints that visited Inveraray castle in 1958 and photocopied the extensive Campbell records. This will bring a nod to any person deeply involved in family history as the Mormon Library in Salt Lake City, Utah is the mecca of many a family historian. In these Campbell transcripts, I found a genealogy of Ailean Mac Eáin. It was not the normal Gaelic medieval genealogy showing a dubious lineage back to Irish kings, but rather just the generations that had dealings with the Campbells. The genealogy started with Eáin Riabhach and then went to his son Ailean Mac Eáin and then to his descendants for several generations. They were all listed under the surname of "Maclachlan," which was the clan of Ailean Mac Eáin. The habit of using a clan surname instead of the patronymic surname of a family is not unusual in scholarly writing about Gaelic families in both Ireland and Scotland. It is convenient for the historian, but can be confusing when looking at documents from the 1500s as the surname a family actually used could change as it followed patronymic patterns.

This genealogy in the Campbell records became my Rosetta stone. The Campbell records listed Duncan Roy McCain as "Duncan Maclachlan." I was able to locate the people and events that appeared in the Campbell genealogy in the actual primary sources. All became clear as I discovered that the descendants listed in the Campbell records as Maclachlan were, in fact, the same people I had found in other records under different surnames and that several of the families used the surname McCain. Many of these sources included these families listed by their derbhfine or gelfine surnames, making it possible to confirm their connection to Ailean Mac Eáin.

The descendants of Ailean Mac Eáin were lords with their own lands in the 1400s and 1500s within the Clann Lachlainn structure. Clann Lachlainn's main lands and the home of their chief were to the east of Kilmichael Glassary parish on the other side of Loch Fyne at Strathlachlan in Cowal. It is only a couple miles across the narrow sea loch from Strathlachan to Kilmichael Glassary parish. The Mac Lachlainns had some presence in Kilmichael Glassary from the 1200s, but the story of the McCains starts with the charter to Ailean Mac Eáin. The *Poltalloch Writs* record on 20 October 1436 that Eáin Mac Lachlainn, taoiseach of Clann Lochlainn, gave a charter to lands in Glassary and the titles of Taoiseach and Seneschal of those lands to his cousin, Ailean Mac Eáin.[23] *Cousin* was often used in a loose sense in Gaelic culture and the exact relationship between Ailean and the chief of Clann Lachlainn is not known.

Modern historians call the family of Ailean Mac Eáin in the aggregate the Mac Lachlainns of Dunadd though in reality only one of his sons was "of Dunadd." A more accurate term would be the Mac Lachlainns of Glassary. They were comprised of four Houses established by the sons of Ailean. I will use Gaelic spellings for the sons because of the total lack of consistency in anglicized forms in the records. I will also include a numerical reference in front of the name of each son to lessen the confusion. The Houses were 1) Dónall of Dunadd, 2) Donnchadh Rua of Dunamuck, 3) Eáin Riabhach of

---

[23] H W Forsyth Harwood ed., 'Extracts from Poltalloch Writs;' *The Genealogist,* vol. 38, (London: G Bell & Sons, Ltd., 1922), 71.

Killinochonoch, and 4) Giolla Chríost of Creag an Tairbh. The Dunamuck House was our Duncan Roy McCain.

The location of the four Houses was important because in the primary sources the House name was often included as a way to identify a family within the group. The attachment of a derbhfine or a gelfine surname and a geographic tag made it possible to follow the descendants of each House. Certain ancestral forenames appear often in the family, such as Eáin Riabhach and Giolla Chríost. Even with the same forenames being used by the four families, a line could be identified if the House name was also included.

The Mac Lachlainns of Glassary appear in multiple primary sources including the *Poltalloch Writs*, the *Inventory of Lamont Papers*, the *Inventory of Scrymgeour Papers*, the *Notary Book of Gavin Hamiltoun*, and the *Argyll Charters*, just to name a few. These records show lands being granted and resigned, clan positions being confirmed, and legal matters dealing with feuds and disputes. The records confirmed that the Houses of the four sons did use some of the surnames in the Mid Argyll Kinship group and some descendants of Duncan Roy McCain were using McCain as a surname. I also confirmed that several of the families in the Mid Argyll Kinship Group were connected to the lands of Ailean Mac Eáin and his sons. These primary sources, along with the DNA confirmation of kinship to families living on Ailean Mac Eáin's lands, made an impressive case that some of his descendants had been located and included my McCains.[24]

---

[24] *Mid Argyll Kinship DNA Project*,
http://www.familytreedna.com/public/MidArgyllKinshipGroup/default.aspx
.

The descendants of the four Houses established by Ailean Mac Eáin can be followed from the early 1500s into the 1800s. By the mid-1600s, they are often recorded by the surname of Mac Lachlainn in official records, but in some cases under the surname McCain and often with an "alias Mac Lachlainn" attached in the record.

The Mac Lachlainns of Glassary were traditional Gaels. As a clan, they came out with the Cowal Mac Lachlainns in 1745 to support Bonnie Prince Charlie to the bitter end at Culloden Moor. Among the descendants of Ailean Mac Eáin, it was normally the oldest son's family of each House that used Mac Lachlainn as a surname as it was their title. Younger sons of these families had to make out as best they could. In the 1700s, these younger sons often entered the army or became lawyers or merchants in English or Scottish cities and other parts of the world. Earlier, however, in the 1500s, this meant going abroad as Redshanks, which is relevant to the McCains and their move to Ireland.

The question of deep ancestry was beyond the goal of my research, but I will offer a few observations. The late Medieval Gaelic genealogies tie Ailean Mac Eáin of Glassary to the Clann Lachlainn in Cowal. Ailean was said to be a cousin to the Cowal Mac Lachlainn chief, but as mentioned, in the Gaelic world a "cousin" could be literal or a polite term referring to some distant relationship of even a maternal line. An example of the use of this term in 1560 is seen when the fifth Earl of Argyll issued a Bond of Maintenance to Archibald Mac Lachlan, then chief of his clan, and addressed him as his "cusing (sic) and servant." In fact, the two men were only distantly related through maternal lines. While the true connection between Ailean Mac Eáin and the Cowal Mac Lachlainn chief is not known, it is not too difficult to place them in a historical context.

The Mac Lachlainn genealogy goes back to a pivotal figure of Giolla Chríost who lived in the 1200s.[25] He had three sons. One of these sons, Giolla Padraig, was the progenitor of the Cowal Clann Lachlainn. His other two sons, Giolla Easpuig and Eoghann, had lands in Glassary. The descendants of Giolla Easpuig and Eoghann eventually lost their lands in Glassary to the Scrymgeour family. In the late-1200s, Giolla Easpuig's line failed to produce a male heir and their lands went to Ralf of Dundee by marriage. The lands of Eoghann were held by his son named Eáin, which passed to his sons by the 1340s. In 1346, the Scottish Crown forfeited the Glassary lands of Eáin's sons to Gilbert of Glassary, who was a grandson of Ralf of Dundee. So by the late 1300s, Gilbert of Glassary had acquired, technically that is, much of the lands of the descendants of Giolla Easpuig and Eoghann, the two sons Giolla Chríost. However, Gilbert of Glassary produced no male heirs and in the 1370s all of these lands went to Alexander Scrymgeour, who had married Agnes, the daughter and heiress of Gilbert of Glassary.

How much control the Scrymgeour family had over the lands that had belonged to Giolla Easpuig and Eoghann Mac Giolla Chríost is questionable. This is a very gray area of Scottish history. At this time, Glassary was the epicenter of the Redshanks society. Redshanks were a warrior class in high demand as mercenaries in Scotland, Ireland, and Europe. They were a law unto themselves. They did no manual labor and

---

[25] See Giolla Chríost Geneology on page 4.

were supported by the tenants of the lord, a practice called "sorning." One sixteenth-century Scottish observer complained that the Glassary Redshanks were, "wild men who cannot be coerced or punished by secular judge or power."[26] The local lore says, and it is probably correct, that the descendants of Eáin son of Eoghann Mac Gilla Chríost took the "clan" surname of their cousins, the Mac Lachlainns of Cowal, and remained on their lands in Glassary. It is also remembered that the Scrymgeours, quite wisely, made no changes and did not require rents, per se. Given the remoteness of mid Argyll and the warlike nature of the local Gaels, the Scrymgeours showed wisdom. The status of land possession in Glassary becomes clearer when a "McCain" family appears there in the 1430s and we are told they are of Clann Lachlainn.

In 1432, a John M'Ean appears in the Glassary writs selling a tract of land at Kilmun in Cowal to John Scrymgeour, son of Alexander. In the writs, we are told John M'Ean's uncle is Giolla Easpuig M'Ean, showing us they both were known by the same surname.[27] Then four years later, Ailean Mac Eáin received a grant to extensive lands in Glassary which included many of the lands that had been held by Giolla Easpuig and Eoghann, the two sons of Giolla Chríost. Ailean Mac Eáin's son, Duncan Roy, is also listed as "McCain" in the 1400s. In other words, a McCain family appears on the scene in the 1430s in control of the lands held by Giolla Chríost's two sons in Glassary. Alastair Campbell of Airds, the Officer of Arms of Scotland and historian, noticed the appearance in Glassary of these McCains in his book *The History of Clan Campbell*.

---

[26] Heather Frances James, *Medieval Rural Settlement, a study of Mid-Argyll, Scotland,* (PhD thesis, University of Glasgow) 124.
[27] JRN MacPhail, 175.

When writing about the sale of land by John M'Ean to Sir John Scrymgeour he noted, "the lands of Kilmun presumably held by the MacIans or MaKanes, whoever they may have been."[28] Mac Phail, the editor of the *The Highland Papers*, also noticed this McCain group and observed they were probably descendants of Giolla Easpuig Mac Giolla Chríost.[29] I would agree with this observation, but suspect they were the descendants of Eáin the son of Eoghann Mac Giolla Chríost. This is why they were known in Gaelic as the Mac Eáin family. The salient point is that, from the early 1430s onward, there was a McCain family and Ailean Mac Eáin and his son Duncan Roy McCain were part of this family.

Much of the history can be deduced from the lands themselves. Several of the Glassary lands that Eoghann and his brother Giolla Easpuig held are the same ones granted to Ailean Mac Eáin in 1436 and later held by his sons. Put into a historical context, the 1400s were a golden age for the local Gaelic powers in mid Argyll and Eáin Mac Lachlainn's grant to Ailean Mac Eáin reflects this. There may have been *official* land resignations, but the reality was Clann Lachlainn still retained control of much of their ancestral lands in Glassary and the 1436 grant confirms this.

By the late 1500s, McCain was *fixed* as a surname. This was almost certainly done to distinguish them as the line of Ailean Mac Eáin. This use of the surname was noticed by local historian Herbert Campbell in the 1922, volume 38 edition of *The Genealogist*. As he put it, "it is practically sure

---

[28] Alastair Campbell, *The History of Clan Campbell, Volume I, From Origins to Flodden,* (Edinburg, Edinburg University Press, 2000) 127.
[29] MacPhail, 225,226.

that two of the three Johns nicknamed 'reoch' belonged to the Dunadd line, so that it looks as though the family were playing with the nickname."[30] "John Reoch" was Campbell's way of anglicizing Eáin Riabhach. He was correct. The name was being used more at that time. An example of what Herbert Campbell meant is seen in the name of Giolla Easpuig Mac Eáin Riabhach Mhic Dhonnchaidh Rua Mhic Lachlainn, who appears in the Lamont Papers in 1612. This derbhfine name would be Archibald McCain in today's English (the lovely Gaelic name Giolla Easpuig is often crudely anglicized as Archibald, it means *servant of the bishop*). In 1570, Alexander M'Ean of Glassary held the lands at Bormolloch. Bormolloch is the farmstead to the immediate east of Creag an Tairbh. Significantly, Alexander M'Ean is listed in the Scrymgeour family records showing yet another connection between these two families.[31] One Campbell tacsman listed in the year 1603 is "John M'Donald V'Ean, alias M'Loauchlan."[32] In Gaelic, his name was Eáin Mac Dónaill Mhic Eáin. The "alias M'Loauchlan" means simply *also known as Mac Lachlainn*. In 1705, another example of the multiple surname use is recorded in the Argyll justiciary records, with "Duncan Vc Lauchlane alias McEan."[33] These are examples of a clerk feeling the need to clarify a McCain's clan affiliation.

The other Mac Eáin families in Argyll also began using fixed forms of their surname in the 1600s. In Glencoe, the Mac

---

[30] Harwood,"Poltalloch Writs", 71.
[31] J Maitland Thomson, ed., *Inventory of Documents Relating to the Scrymgeour Family Estates 1611* (Edinburgh: J Skinner and Company, 1912), 24.
[32] Innes, *Parochiales,* 165. Taken from the Brendalbane Charters.
[33] John Cameron, ed., *The Justiciary Records of Argyll and the Isles 1664-1705, Volume 1*(Edinburgh, The Stair Society), 75.

Eáins were known as the Mac Eáin Abarach family. *Abarach* means "bold" or "courageous." It was used to indicate which Mac Eáin family they were, just as the Dunamuck Mac Eáins used the suffix Riabhach. In the records during the 1500s and early 1600s, the Glencoe Mac Eáins are often listed as "M'Ean Abrych." As with the Mac Eáin family of Dunamuck, the epithet signifying the House was eventually dropped and they were known as the McCains of Glencoe. This is one reason why researchers centuries later confused the Glassary McCains with the Glencoe McCains. They assumed all McCains were from the more famous Glencoe brand.

One of the Mid Argyll Kinship surnames had an interesting link to the Ailean Mac Eáin family. In the case of Mac Ailpin, there was a geographic connection to Ailean Mac Eáin. On 4 January 1608, in the *Poltalloch Writs* recorded at Inveraray castle, the Earl of Argyll addressed a *precept of clare constat* to Duncan McAlpine in Garbhallt.[34] Garbhallt was the land of 2) Donnchadh Rua Mac Eáin. It could be that this Mac Ailpín line comes from a son of 2) Donnchadh Rua's line or perhaps a younger son of one of his descendants who was named Ailpín. The McAlpin families that participated in the DNA test were from the Loch Ederline area, which is on the southern end of Loch Awe within minutes of both Garbhallt and Bormolloch.

The Kilmichael Glassary Mac Ailpins are a prolific family. One branch of this Mac Ailpin family migrated to County Mayo in the west of Ireland in the 1790s and produced several Roman Catholic notables, including Monsignor Patrick McAlpine, who in the late 1800s was parish priest and vicar

---

[34] Ibid., 142.

general in Clifden, County Galway. Two other Church notables from their family were Reverend Father Francis McAlpine and Sister Ellen Mary McAlpine. The nephew of Monsignor Patrick McAlpine was important in Mississippi history. He was the pastor at the Church of the Sacred Heart in Biloxi, Mississippi from 1939 to 1967. It is an interesting coincidence that both the McCains and McAlpins played a part in Mississippi history.

The Henry families provide the largest number of DNA matches in the Mid Argyll Kinship Group outside of McCains. Many of these Henry families eventually settled in Ireland in the Bann Valley on the border of Counties Antrim and Derry. Their surname in Gaelic is Mac Eanruig. There was a historical Mac Eanruig family associated with Loch Awe on the northern part of Kilmichael Glassary. However, there is no known connection between them and Ailean Mac Eáin. The Henry DNA match is more distant than the other families in the Mid Argyll Kinship Group. It is possible that the Henry families hold a key to the deep ancestry of the family of Ailean Mac Eáin. If the Henry families in the Mid Argyll Kinship Group are the historical Henry family of Loch Awe, that would be significant and provide insight into many of the old ruling families in mid Argyll.

I was satisfied that our McCains were descended from Ailean Mac Eáin and our family was *the* McCain family in the Glassary records in the 1400s onward. My next goal was to find out what caused the family to move from Kilmichael Glassary to east Donegal. The Campbells and their intrigues in Ulster were the vector. The four Houses of Ailean Mac Eáin's sons were allied to the powerful Earls of Argyll of Clan

Campbell. The fifth Earl, Giolla Easpuig Donn Caimbeul, orchestrated a movement of Gaels from Kilmichael Glassary to east Donegal. This gave me a trail to follow.

For those readers who would like to delve deeper into the descendants of Ailean Mac Eáin as they appear in the primary sources, I include several paragraphs on the four Houses established by his sons. Their names are listed in documents in a complex mixture of Lallans influenced English and phonetic Gaelic. I have left some of the names as they appear in the original documents and others I have put into Gaelic. These paragraphs are optional and will make little sense to the reader not familiar with Gaelic society of the 1500s. It is perfectly acceptable to stop here and proceed to the next chapter where the general narrative continues, but for the hard-core, I provide this interesting data.

*****

Notes on the four Houses established by the sons of Ailean Mac Eáin:

1) Dónall of Dunadd

The family of 1) Donáll was the ruling line of the Mac Lachlainns of Glassary. In primary sources, they are listed by several surnames that follow Gaelic patronymic customs and often their clan name of Mac Lachlainn is not present in early records. Descendants of Dónall are referred to as "the Mac Lachlainns of Dunadd" to separate them from the Houses established by his three brothers.

One of 1) Dónall's sons and his heir was named Ailean. This Ailean's son was Dónall named after his grandfather. This

Dónall married Fionnuala Nic Eáin (Nic is the feminine form of Mac). This same Dónall and his wife Fionnuala are in both the Campbell genealogy of Ailean Mac Eáin and in the land records of the parish. In the Campbell genealogy, this Dónall is listed under the surname Mac Lachlainn, but in the notary book his surname is recorded as Mac Ailein. This is an example of how the surname of the family would be different depending on the focus and intent of the writer. In this case, the surname Mac Ailein is rendered Mac Lachlainn by modern writers. In the *Notary Book of Gavin Hamiltoun* there is this entry:

> ...In the same year (1572) Finvall Nikean, the wife of Donald M'Alane V'Donile of Dunnad, resigned to James Scrymgeoure of Dudhope constable of Dundee the twenty shillinglands of Carnyame, the said Donald warranting the constable free of all harm in respect of the lands from the heirs of the deceased Lauchlane M'Donald V'Alane.[35]

In the passage above, the name Donald M'Alane V'Donile of Dunadd is in Gaelic, Dónall Mac Ailein Mhic Dhónaill of Dunadd. Mhic is used in Gaelic surnames to signify a grandson of, but occasionally as a clan surname. In English this name is, Donald son of Ailean the grandson of Donald. This surname establishes a clear line of descent from 1) Dónall, son of Ailean Mac Eáin. The deceased Lauchlane M'Donald V'Alane is the uncle of Donald M'Alane V'Donile of Dunnad.

---

[35] Cosmo Nelson Innes ed., and others, *Origines* Parochiales *Scotiae*, vol. 2, pt 1, (Edinburgh: The Bannatyne Club, 1854), 48.

The clerk supplies the House name of Dunadd leaving absolutely no doubt about the family's identity.

Fionnuala Nic Eáin was certainly a cousin to Dónall as her surname is the feminine form of Mac Eáin. It is significant that Fionnuala Nic Eáin is listed by her own surname. In the Gaelic world this meant she was important and probably had property rights in Kilmichael Glassary. Fionnuala Nic Eáin is the only woman listed in the entire genealogy provided by Sir Ian Douglas Campbell of Ailean Mac Eáin's family. One day I hope to uncover more of her story, as it must be an interesting one. There may be, in some dusty library, some record not yet located that would reveal all. Also of interest in the record above is yet another link between the Scrymgeour family and the descendants of Ailean Mac Eáin.

The descendants of 1) Dónall appear many times in the *Poltalloch Writs*. These writs record title deeds in private ownership in mid Argyll and record the awarding of offices and similar matters. Some examples of 1) Dónall's family in the writs:

> At Castle Lachlan, 24 Nov 1502 Sasine … of the office of Seneschal of all his lands west of Lochfyne given by John Maclachlan of Strathlachlan to his cousin, Donald, son of Allan Maclachlan. Witnesses: the Earl of Argyll

> 29 Sept 1533 Sasine … of lands of Dunadd, Kenmore, Stratharthur and Barnakill, given on the said lands by Lachlan Maclachlan of Strathlachlan to Allan McDonill VcAllan

VcLachlan, as son and heir of deceased Donald McAllan MacLachlan. Witnesses: Duncan Roy McAllan Maclachlan, Donald Maclachlan, son and heir apparent of "the Lord Maclachlan," Kanich McAne reoch McAllan Maclachlan, Patrick McDonill McAllan Maclachlan...[36]

Both entries above show the handover of power and lands. The 1502 listing to Dónall after the passing of Ailean, son of 1) Dónall, and the 1533 listing records the handover of land and position to the next generation. A *sasine* is the right of possession of a freehold estate in feudal law. A Seneschal is the position of subchief under the overall chief who was in both entries the chief of Clann Lachlainn. The Seneschal was also the first lord, or *the law*, in the land, and responsible for running the courts and enforcing the laws and feudal wishes of his chief. Of interest, the witnesses include several members from the other Houses established by Ailean Mac Eáin's sons and the son of the chief of Clann Mhic Lachlainn. This confirms the four Houses established by Ailean Mac Eáin's sons were part of Clann Mhic Lachlainn.

Through the land and title grants, the descendants of 1) Dónall can be followed throughout the 1500s well into the 1700s. Some of them used the surnames Mac Dónaill and Mac Ailein, but most in the House used Mac Lachlainn by 1600.

---

[36] Harwood,"Poltalloch Writs", 71.

2) Donnchadh Rua of Dunamuck

2) Donnchadh Rua is the first descendant of Ailean Mac Eáin known to use the surname McCain. 2) Donnchadh Rua's House was also the *maverick* line. They seemed to have an independent streak and to get into trouble as a result, suggestive of McCain characteristics that follow certain lines of the family to this day. Donnchadh Rua's burial slab includes a magnificent Gaelic sword, very ornate Celtic interweaving patterns, and lion icons. A sword on a Gaelic burial slab signified a lord of high standing from a military family and this House provided Redshanks and captains for the Earls of Argyll. The lion is the symbol of the family and was used by the Glassary Mac Lachlainns since the late 1200s.

2) Donnchadh Rua appears in the Exchequer Rolls of Scotland in the year 1468 in a statement of *sasine* as "Duncan McKane" of Torran, Corblaren, and Garbhallt.[37] All these lands are close to Loch Awe. The next certain mention of him is in 1479 when he was asked by the King of Scotland to resign certain lands, including Garbhallt and Craignure, to Cailean Caimbeul, the Earl of Argyll. Garbhallt is just to the east of Loch Ederline and south of Loch Awe. Craignure is a short distance southeast of Garbhallt. 2) Donnchadh Rua's name is recorded in 1479 as Duncan Makeane.[38] 2) Donnchadh Rua is listed as "of Dunamuck" in the Campbell records and his line is often qualified with this geographic tag. Dunamuck is a settlement about one mile to the west of Kilmichael Glassary village where 2) Donnchadh Rua's burial stone is located.

---

[37] George Burnett, ed., *Exchequer Rolls of Scotland*, vol. IX, (Edinburgh: H M General Register House, 1886).
[38] Innes, *Parochiales,* 46, (transcript from the Argyll Charters).

Incidentally, when a lord resigned his lands over to another lord, he did not necessarily lose them. The practice was often used to establish an overlord and the lands were then given back to the holder, but with obligations of military service and taxes to be paid to the new overlord. In this case, over lordship of these specific lands changed from the chief of the Mac Lachlainns of Cowal to the Earl of Argyll, the chief of the Campbells.

2) Donnchadh Rua's last appearance in the records is on 11 September 1511, when the *Poltalloch Writs* record Duncan roy MacLachlan in Stirling acting as a witness on behalf of the Earl of Argyll concerning a *precept of sasine* to give lands to the Earl's sublords.[39] The Rua or "Roy" epithet appears in the gelfine of 2) Donnchadh Rua's sons and grandsons throughout the 1500s. *Precept of sasine* was an order to preside over a ceremony giving heritable lands to a vassal.

2) Donnchadh Rua's oldest son and heir was Lachlann Mac Donnchaidh Rua. He appears in the *Poltalloch Writs* on 20 October 1547 in connection with a *precept of clare constat*.[40] His name is written "Lachlan McDonche VcAllan of Dunemuck." This gelfine surname and geographic tag confirms this Lachlann's ancestry to Donnchadh Rua, but in this case Mhic Ailein is listed showing Lachlan's grandfather. A *precept of clare constat* was the ceremony to confirm heritable lands to the heir of a deceased vassal. Dunemuck is an older anglicized form of the modern Dunamuck. In Gaelic, it is Dun na Muice, meaning in English the *fort of the pig*.

---

[39] Harwood, "Poltalloch Writs", 183.
[40] Ibid., 139.

On 28 July 1569, a *precept of sasine* was given by Giolla Easpuig Donn Caimbeul, the fifth Earl of Argyll, to Lachlan McDonchie of Dunemuck and his son, Duncan.[41] On 6 May 1563, another descendant, Allane M'Ane V'Conache Roy, shows up in the records as a witness to a contract of Protection and Manrent to Cailean Caimbeul, the chief of the Glen Orchy Campbells.[42] The Glen Orchy Campbells, to the north of Loch Awe, were in a brutal clan war with the famous MacGregors. Cailean Caimbeul's kinsman, the fifth Earl of Argyll, gave support to the Glen Orchy Campbells. Allane M'Ane V'Conache Roy in Gaelic is Ailean Mac Eáin Mhic Donnchaidh Rua, and this gelfine name tells us he was a grandson of 2) Donnchadh Rua. Several of the Mac Lachlainns of Glassary acted on behalf of the Campbells during their war with the MacGregors in the 1560s. This again shows the Dunamuck House as part of the Campbell network of allies in the 1500s. Mid Argyll, under the influence of Earls of Argyll, was governed through a hybrid traditional Gaelic and late feudal system. The fifth Earl of Argyll was the most powerful feudal lord in Argyll and, indeed, was one of the most powerful men in Scotland. He is also important to the McCain story, as will be discussed later.

In the *Poltalloch Writs* on 3 August 1569, Lachlan McDonchie of Dunemuck is listed once again, but this time his full name appears "Lachlan McDonchie roy VcAllan of Dunemuck," in Gaelic, Lachlann Mac Donnchaidh Rua Mhic

---

[41] Ibid.
[42] Innes, Cosmo Nelson, ed., *The Black Book of Taymouth* (Edinburgh, 1855), 208.

Ailein. The full surname given in the 1569 *sasine* document identifies this line as that of 2) Donnchadh Rua.[43]

In Kirnan on 19 December 1572, a rare female of his family is recorded. Her name was Aifric Nic Dhonnchaidh Rua and she was the wife of James Scrymgeour of Dudhope. On that date, James and his wife resigned lands they held in order that they be re-granted to their son and heir, Malcolm Scyrmgeour.[44]

In 1579, a Lachlann Mac Lachlainn of Dunamuck killed Robert Lamont of Silvercraigs.[45] This Lachlann is a descendant of 2) Donnchadh Rua, perhaps the Lachlann that appeared in the 1569 sasine, but possibly a son of his. Either way, the geographic tag confirms the House. To prevent further bloodshed, the Dunamuck family gave certain lands to James Lamont of Inveryne, who was the chief of the Lamont clan. James Lamont was married to a Mac Lachlainn.[46] The exchange of lands and in-law relationship did prevent an all-out feud, but left the Dunamuck House somewhat poorer. The affair was recorded in *An Inventory of Lamont Papers* with his clan name being used:

10 January 1580-81.

Letters of Procurators by Lachlan Mak Lachlane of that Ilk, for resigning in the hands of the King, his five merk lands of Enochan, in favour of, and for new infeftment thereof to be

---

[43] Harwood, *Poltolloch Writs*, 139.
[44] Harwood, *Poltalloch Writs*, 144.
[45] Sir Norman Lamont, ed., *Inventory of Lamont Papers*, (Edinburgh: J Skinner & Co. Ltd., 1914), 126.
[46] Ibid., 99.

given to, James Lamonthe of Inneryn in implement of contract entered into between the late Archibald Mak Lachlane of that Ilk on one part and the said James Lamonthe on the other part, and that in part satisfaction of the slaughter of the late Robert Lamonthe of Silvercraigs, committed suddenly by Lachlan Maklachlan of Dunnemvcke. Dated at Dumbertane 10th January 1580-81. "Witnesses, Mr Duncan Mak Lachlane paternal uncle of the resigner, Duncan M'Donill vic Lachlan of Dunnad, John M 'Lachlan leiche of Ardin, Adam Kammro oig M'Kanniche vic Lachlan of Culzemichand, Dougall Mak Cleriche of Bralekane, Mr. William Houstoun.[47]

Also of interest in this record of the Lamont incident was the appearance of kinsmen from the three other Mac Lachlainn Houses in Kilmichael Glassary as witnesses in the settlement. The ridiculously anglicized geographic name *Culzemichand* is Killnochonoch, which I will discuss later. The John M'Lachlan leiche above is of the House of 4) Giolla Chríost.

In 1612, another group of Mac Lachlainns are in the Lamont Papers who appear to be more of 2) Donnchadh Rua's descendants. This source is particularly information rich as the full derbhfine surname form was used. On 14 January of that year, Archibald M'Eane reoch Vc Donchie roy Vc Lachlane (in Gaelic, Giolla Easpuig Mac Eáin Riabhach Mhic Dhonnchaidh Rua Mhic Lochlainn), of Shirvan was made *principal* to Walter

---

[47] Lamont, *Inventory,* 99.

Lamont son of John Lamont of Anaskeog. The Cautioners listed were Giolla Easpuig Mac Dónaill Mhic Dhonnchaidh Rua Mhic Lachlainn and Lachlan Mac Dónaill Mhic Dhonnchaidh Rua Mhic Lachlainn.[48] The two Cautioners and the Principal carry the identifying "Mhic Dhonnchaidh Rua" in their name, which is also used in the 1569 *sasine* document concerning 2) Donnchadh Rua's son and grandson.

The descendants of 2) Donnchadh Rua are less numerous in the records than the other three Houses in the 1600s and by 1700 the land is owned by other families. However, they are found from time to time. An example is "John M'Viccane," a land holder in Rhudil (adjacent to Shirvan listed above) in 1672, which was a holding of this family.[49] The name in Gaelic is Eáin Mac Mhic Eáin, which is a "clan" surname form of Mac Eáin and an example of this House using McCain as a surname. Given the lack of a standard surname orthography and the span of chronology involved it is not possible to construct an exact genealogy for 2) Donnchadh Rua, even having this much information. However, from the residences mentioned and the Gaelic custom of listing partial genealogies in surnames, at least some of the descendants of 2) Donnchadh Rua can be accounted for and they did use McCain as a surname.

3) Eáin Riabhach of Killinochonoch

3) Eáin Riabhach is listed in the Campbell genealogies as "of Killienuchanoch," which is a crudely anglicized form of

---

[48] Lamont, *Inventory*, 99.
[49] JRN MacPhail, ed., Highland *Papers Volume II* (Edinburgh: University Press, 1916), 215.

a lovely Gaelic place name meaning *the moaning wood*. I am not certain of the Scots Gaelic, but the Ulster Gaelic I speak would make it Coille a' Chaointe. Killinochonoch is the modern anglicized form and it is located less than three miles northwest of Dunadd. The grandson of 3) Eáin Riabhach is listed in the Poltalloch Writs on 2 October 1581 as "Kannich oig McKannych Vc Ane Reoch;" in Gaelic, Coinneach Óg Mac Coinnigh Mhic Eáin Riabhach.[50] This Coinneach was the Baillie, or magistrate, for the Mac Lachlainn chief. On that date, Coinneach Óg performed a *sasine* to give Shirvan Mill to Donnchadh Mac Dónaill Mhic Ailein of Dunadd, son and heir of the deceased Dónaill Mac Lachlainn of Dunadd. This confirmed the connection of this House to 3) Eáin Riabhach, that their main residence was in Killinochonoch, and that the head of the Killinochonoch House was a Baillie for the chief of Clann Lachlainn.

Another descendant of 3) Eáin Riabhach is listed in the Lamont Papers on 10 January 1581 by the crudely anglicized name Adam Kammro oig M'Kanniche Vic Lachland.[51] The "Kammro" is difficult to decipher, but the rest of his name links him to Coinneach the son of 3) Eáin Riabhach. These variations in the surnames forms are typical in Argyll in the sixteenth-century. In this case, 3) Eáin Riabhach's name is omitted and the clan name is given.

4) Giolla Chríost of Creag an Tairbh

North of Killinochonoch is Creag an Tairbh, which is the name of a rocky hill and settlement to the immediate west

---

[50] Harwood,"Poltalloch Writs", 72.
[51] Lamont, *Inventory*, 99.

of Loch Awe and near the western shore of Loch Ederline. Creag an Tairbh was the location of the House of 4) Giolla Chríost. The Creag an Tairbh family were hereditary physicians to the Campbell family in the 1500s and 1600s. On 4 August 1552, "John Leche, a Mac Lochlainn" of Creag an Tairbh made a bond with Cailean Caimbeul.[52] Leche is the Lallans word for physician, from the word *leech*, the blood sucking annelids which were a tool of the medical trade in those days. In Gaelic, physician is Leagha and the surname form is Mac an Leagha which is anglicized as MacLea, yet another name in the Mid Argyll Kinship group. This line appears several times with their physician status noted. Colin Leche MacLachlan was a physician to the fifth Earl of Argyll, Giolla Easpuig Donn Caimbeul, and later to his half-brother, Cailean Caimbeul, the sixth Earl of Argyll.[53]

Another descendant of 4) Giolla Chríost was Eáin Mac Giolla Chríost Mhic Ailein Mhic Lachlainn, who is in the Campbell records and in the *Poltalloch Writs*. Eáin Mac Giolla Chríost was a witness to a *sasine* ceremony on 29 September 1533.[54] Once again, a partial genealogy is included in his name allowing him to be identified. On the 17 January 1600 entry of the Poltalloch Writs, Archibald Leitche of Strones is a witness to a charter at Kilmartin, but noted as being "a Mac Lachlainn."[55] In the 1672 Glassary writs, Mac an Leagha

---

[52] Jane E A Dawson, *Campbell Letters* (Edinburgh: Scottish Historical Society, 1997), 78.
[53] Ibid., 42.
[54] Harwood,"Poltalloch Writs", 71.
[55] Ibid., 185.

appears in the semi anglicized forms as "M'Inleitch and M'Ialich."[56]

After the Earls of Argyll extended their lordship over much of Kilmichael Glassary, the Creag an Tairbh House became not only physicians, but also tacsmen and captains for the Campbells. Tacsman (in Gaelic, *Fear Taic*) was a Scottish legal status where a man held land for the lord. The tacsman would let out this land to sub-tenants, keeping some land for himself. In his 1775 *A Journey to the Western Islands of Scotland,* Dr. Johnson described them:

> Next in dignity to the laird is the Tacksman (sic); a large taker or lease-holder of land, of which he keeps part as a domain in his own hand, and lets part to under-tenants. The tacksman is necessarily a man capable of securing to the laird the whole rent, and is commonly a collateral relation. These tacks, or subordinate possessions, were long considered as hereditary, and the occupant was distinguished by the name of the place at which he resided. He held a middle station, by which the highest and the lowest orders were connected. He paid rent and reverence to the laird, and received them from the tenants.

The tacsmen were often blood relations of the chief, but also non-related families would become tacsmen. The Campbells were politically astute and incorporated in-laws and gentry of

---

[56] MacPhail, 214, 217.

the clans they were allied with into these lucrative and important positions.

The ruling line of the House of Creag an Tairbh daughtered out eventually, that is to say, the family produced no male heirs. When Colin MacLachlan of Creag an Tairbh died in 1804, his heir was his daughter, Lucy, wife of Archibald Bell, a writer in Inveraray. Archibald Bell and his two sons changed their surname to MacLachlan to preserve the *title*. The Creag an Tairbh family did establish other branches of their House in Innis Chonaill, Kilmelford, Kilbride, and Lismore.

The Campbells

The McCains were living in mid Argyll, in the parish of Kilmichael Glassary, in the 1500s. They left Argyll for Ireland sometime after 1569 and they were probably of the House Dunamuck established by Duncan Roy McCain. This House had links to the Earl of Argyll of Clan Campbell and he was the catalyst for the move. Perhaps it was the killing of the Lamont of Silvercraigs that encouraged them to migrate or perhaps they were just fulfilling their military obligation to the Campbells. Whatever the case, the McCains migrated from Kilmichael Glassary and settled in east Donegal. The historical events around this migration are remarkable and read like some romantic historical fiction, but it is all true.

Clan Campbell was a powerful Highland Scottish family who extended their influence into Ulster in the 1500s with a profound effect on not only Ulster, but all of Ireland. The chief of Clan Campbell in the mid-1500s was the dynamic fifth Earl of Argyll, Giolla Easpuig Donn Caimbeul. His first cousin was Fionnuala Níc Dhónaill, who is famous in Ireland to this day and is better known by her nickname, Iníon Dubh (black haired daughter). It was on her lands that the McCains first appear in Donegal.

The movement of Scots to Ulster during the Plantation is a well-known event. It began in 1609 and ebbed and flowed throughout the 1600s into the early 1700s. Most of this migration came from the Scottish Lowlands. However, there were other migrations of Scots into Ulster. The first migration was the Gallóglaigh families that came from Argyll and the Hebrides. Their migration began in the late 1200s and continued throughout the 1300s. The Gallóglaigh were a hereditary warrior caste. In time, they became clans with their own lands throughout Ireland. The second migration also came from Argyll and the Hebrides. These Scots were called Redshanks. They were from the same Scottish families as the Gallóglaigh, but they functioned differently in Irish society. Irish historian G. A. Hayes-McCoy says of them, "… they remained distinct from the older Gallóglaigh families, and they did not settle in Ireland."[57] The last part of that quote is in error however, as by the mid-1500s many of the Redshanks did settle in Ireland.

The Redshanks were hired as mercenaries in great numbers by various Irish lords in Ulster and in general they did return home to Scotland after the summer campaign season. This was not always the case, however, and there were Redshanks settling in Ulster as early as the late 1300s. By the mid-1500s, political and military conditions in Ulster had changed and even more Redshanks settled in north Antrim and other places, such as Donegal. Scottish historian, Wilson McLeod, addresses this migration in his book *Divided Gaels* by amending Hays-McCoy's migration paradigm to include a

---

[57] Wilson McLeod, *Divided Gaels: Gaelic Cultural Identities in Scotland and Ireland c. 1200-1650*, (Oxford: Oxford University Press, 2004), 41.

"fourth movement," which he describes as being "less tangible from the historical records but nevertheless of considerable significance."[58] McLeod asserts this movement took place from the fourteenth to sixteenth centuries. It included the movement of Clan Donald into north Antrim as well as the Scots who came from the Campbell lands in Argyll and settled in Donegal. It is the latter that concerns the McCains.

In the 1500s, Clan Campbell was arguably the most important Gaelic family of their age, both in Ireland and Scotland. They recognized the changing world of the early modern period and adjusted to it. Their chiefs were the Earls of Argyll and they provided effective leadership for their clan. The Campbells were old order traditional Gaels in every sense, but they operated and thought outside the Gaelic world. Under the leadership of the Earls of Argyll, the clan established cadet families in the Scottish Lowlands and they had a presence in the Scottish Court in Edinburgh. The sons of the clan's gentry received formal training in the Gaelic tradition, but also went to universities in the Lowlands. The Earls established trading houses in Scotland and England. The Earls of Argyll and their court were tri-lingual and could communicate in Gaelic, Lallans, and Latin. The Earls patronized the Gaelic arts and there were the great poets, men of letters, and musicians, from Ireland and the Scottish Gaeltacht, at the Earls' court, and yet at the same time Lowland artisans and craftsmen were also in residence there. The Earls were patrons of Bishop John Carswell, known in Argyll as Seon Carsuel. In 1567, with Campbell patronage, he produced a translation of the *Book of Common Order*, or *Foirm na nUrrnuidheadh*, which was the

---

[58] Ibid.

first book printed in the Gaelic language. The House of Campbell was a powerful and dynamic force in the Gaelic world and beyond and in the mid-1500s they turned their considerable influence toward Ulster.

The fifth Earl of Argyll was born in 1538 and was Earl from 1558 until his death in 1573. His accomplishments were many despite his premature death by illness. He held court at Inveraray Castle in mid Argyll. Lord Argyll was a principal player in many of the major events of his day in both Ireland and Scotland. He was an interesting man in many regards. He was a Protestant and an early patron of the Reformed church in the Scottish Gaeltacht, yet at times he also supported the Roman Catholic Mary Queen of Scots. Part of his family business was broker and supplier of Redshanks to the Irish lords in Ulster. In the mid-1500s, the use of Redshank mercenaries by the Irish chiefs in Ulster grew greatly as did their reputation as elite fighting men. By 1575, Redshank pay was equal to that of the famed Gallóglaigh. In 1566, Sir Francis Knollys, an English agent in Ireland, reported to Queen Elizabeth that 300 Redshanks were "harder to be vanquished in battle than 600 Irishmen."[59] The Redshanks were a profitable business for Lord Argyll and one that allowed him to promote his political agenda in Scotland and Ireland.

In 1555, Clan Campbell extended their sphere of influence and operations into Ireland. In Donegal that year, a bitter O'Donnell power struggle erupted between Calbhach Ó Dónaill and his father Manus Ó Dónaill. Calbhach Ó Dónaill travelled to Argyll to meet with the fourth Earl of Argyll to

---

[59] Hans Claude Hamilton, ed., *Calendar of the State Papers Relating to Ireland* (London: Longman, Green, Longman & Roberts, 1860), 302.

negotiate for Campbell Redshanks and military expertise. An agreement was reached and the fourth Earl allowed his son, the young Giolla Easpuig Donn Caimbeul, to lead the expedition. This gave Giolla Easpuig Donn first hand military experience in Ulster. The campaign was a total success and Giolla Easpuig Donn established a long term friendship with Calbhach Ó Dónaill. This friendship and his experience in Ulster would prove important to the future fifth Earl.

The details of how the Campbells were drawn into Ulster reads like a sordid soap opera plot, albeit much more complex. In 1558, the fourth Earl of Argyll died and his son Giolla Easpuig Donn became the fifth Earl of Argyll. His father left a pretty young widow, Giolla Easpuig Donn's stepmother, and she was a powerful woman in her own right. She was Catríona Nic Ghiolla Eáin, the daughter of Eachann Mór Mac Giolla Eáin. Her family was a powerful clan from the Hebrides and they were both allies of the Campbells and suppliers of Redshanks. The Earl had to find a suitable new husband for his stepmother and he had just the man, Calbhach Ó Dónaill, the new chief of the O'Donnell clan. Catríona arrived in Donegal with 2,000 Redshanks accompanying her and, in 1560, she and Cabhlach were wed. The fifth Earl had killed two birds with one stone with the marriage. He reaped a considerable profit of 100 pounds sterling per annum for the Redshanks provided to Calbhach and he allied his house to the O'Donnell clan.[60] The marriage also drew the Earl deeper into Irish politics.

---

[60] Jane E A Dawson, *The Politics of Religion in the Age of Mary Queen of Scots, The Earl of Argyll and the Struggle for Britain and Ireland* (Cambridge: Cambridge University Press, 2002), 106.

The late 1560s were busy times in Ulster. There were clan conflicts and the Elizabethan English were constantly testing the Gaelic defences in Ulster. Things went well for Calbhach at first. In 1561, Calbhach was cooperating with the Elizabethan English in order to strengthen his hold upon his clan. Calbhach's rising status and power was noticed by the great clan O'Neill chief, Seaán Ó Neill (said Shane O'Neal). Seaán was ambitious and commanded the strongest military force in Ulster. He demanded fealty from all the clans in Ulster, including his rivals, the O'Donnells. Calbhach received intelligence that Seaán had entered Tír Chónaill to demand Calbhach's fealty. Calbhach, however, launched a surprise night raid on Seaán's camp killing and capturing many of Seaán's men and sending the rest fleeing into the night, including Seaán himself. This embarrassing defeat did not sit well with Seaán and he managed to enact his revenge later in the year by surprising Calbhach and his wife while they were staying at a monastery in Tír Chónaill. Seaán surrounded the monastery and took both Calbhach and Catríona prisoner.

After the capture, there were rumors that Catríona had become Seaán's sex slave or perhaps mistress. The version of the story that reached Lord Argyll was she was in chains and Seaán was having his way with her often. Lord Argyll considered a rescue attempt, but matters in Scotland kept him occupied and he turned the problem over to the Elizabethan English officials in Ireland, who did absolutely nothing. Losing his patience, Lord Argyll then offered a generous ransom of 300 pounds sterling and 400 Redshanks. This was accepted by Seaán and Calbhach Ó Dónaill was freed in 1564, however, Catríona chose to remain with Seaán, raising more than a few Gaelic eyebrows. She went on to marry Seaán and bore him several sons.

That was not the end of sexual politics in this tale however, as more interesting events loomed ahead. Calbhach plotted his revenge, but years of harsh treatment in Seaan's dungeon had taken its toll and he passed away in 1566. His half-brother, Aodh Mac Manus Ó Dónaill was then inaugurated as The Ó Dónaill. To follow the course of events, it is necessary to go to the previous year when Seaán went to war against his other clan rivals, the Clan Donald in north Antrim. Clan Donald was a pan Gaelic one that held lands in northern Ireland and Scotland. In May of 1565, Seaán defeated them in the battle of Glentaisie in the Glens of Antrim. He captured the Clan Donald chief, Seamus Mac Dónaill, and his brother Somhairle Buí Mac Dónaill, who was the head of the Antrim branch of their clan. In July 1565, Seamus Mac Dónaill died of wounds received in the battle and the harsh treatment during his incarceration. Seamus was married to Anna Caimbeul, the aunt of Giolla Easpuig Donn Caimbeul. Lord Argyll was particularly fond of his aunt and her children, who were now in extreme danger. He had been vexed by Seaán Ó Neill twice now and the matter would escalate.

Campbell women were important assets to their clan. They married important people for important reasons. Anna Caimbeul was the daughter of Cailean Caimbeul, the third Earl of Argyll. Her first marriage to James Stewart of Bute ended in annulment. Her second marriage was to Seamus Mac Dónaill, the Clan Donald chief. They had a successful marriage, producing many children and the MacDonald and Campbell Houses were allied in those days. Anna Caimbeul was very close to her nephew and she relied on him to protect her and her children and to try to free Somhairle Buí Mac Dónaill. This complex situation did partially resolve itself in the spring of 1567.

Seaán Ó Neill, once again, invaded Donegal, and this time he was utterly defeated at the battle of Farsetmore, just north of Letterkenny, on 8 May 1567. It was a large clan battle between Clan O'Donnell under Aodh Mac Manus Ó Dónaill and Clan O'Neill under Seaán Ó Neill. Each side had around 2,000 men, comprised of Irish warriors, Gallóglaigh, and Redshanks. Seaán's army was routed with high casualties. He did manage to escape back across the Foyle River, but Seaán needed troops and needed them fast in case the O'Donnells followed up on their victory, or even worse the English decided to move into his territory. He was desperate and decided to parley with Clan Donald. He wanted to make peace with them and use their Redshanks to defend his home territory.

Seaán's plan involved taking another woman to his bed. He suggested that he was willing to send Catríona back to her father and marry Anna Caimbeul, the widow of Seamus Mac Dónaill. Now, the problem with this plan was obvious. Seaán had killed Anna Caimbeul's husband and she preferred his head on a platter to marriage. Seaán released Somhairle Buí Mac Dónaill and then rode to north Antrim with only his personal bodyguard. He began negotiations with Alasdair Óg Mac Dónaill, the acting head of the Clan Donald and brother of Seamus and Somhairle. Seaán met with Alasdair Óg at Cushendun in the Glens of Antrim, on 31 May 1567. Alasdair Óg was with a body of Redshanks. Many of them had been recruited for him by Lord Argyll. The negotiations would have been difficult for Seaán since he was in a vulnerable position after the near destruction of his army at Farsetmore. Plus, Somhairle Buí was now a free man. Seaán presented his best offer and one he thought generous, to wed and bed Anna, in exchange for a small army of Redshanks. The negotiations did not go well for Seaán.

The death of Seaán Ó Neill came on 2 June 1567. The exact details of his death will never be known, but there were several parties that certainly wanted him dead. Clan Donald wanted revenge and Lord Argyll had been troubled by Seaán on several occasions. The Elizabethan English also would benefit from Seaán's death. The facts are Alasdair Óg, the captain of his Redshanks, and a few chosen warriors walked into a room to *negotiate* with Seaán. When they left the room, the great Irish chief was dead. Of interest, the Captain of Alasdair Óg's Redshanks was named Dónall Mac Eáin.[61] It is speculation, but given the fact that the Earl of Argyll recruited many of Alasdair Óg's Redshanks from his lands in mid-Argyll and that the McCains were linked to the Earl, that this Dónall Mac Eáin was a grandson of Duncan Roy McCain of Dunamuck. I was left with the idea that a McCain may have been the man that assassinated the great Irish chief.

The death of Seaán solved one problem for Lord Argyll and presented him with an opportunity to extend his influence into Ulster. He had a plan for a great Ulster alliance between the clans Campbell, O'Donnell, O'Neill, and MacDonald. Lord Argyll, once again, turned to the women of his clan. He proposed that his Aunt Anna marry the successor to Seaán, who was Tarlach Luimneach Ó Neill, and furthermore, that her

---

[61] Hamilton, *Calendar,* 363.

daughter, Fionnuala Nic Dhónaill, marry the head of the O'Donnells, Aodh Mac Manus Ó Dónaill. It was bold, it was genius, and it worked. All parties agreed and the marriages were set to take place in the summer of 1568. The ease at which the marriages were arranged suggests it was in the planning stages prior to Seaán's death and it is possible that Seaán's murder was part of the plan. However, the marriages were put on hold for a year because matters in Scotland became critical for Lord Argyll.

In Scotland, Lord Argyll's affairs were incredibly complex as he was in the middle of the tumultuous events surrounding Mary Queen of Scots' attempt to hold onto power. Lord Argyll was a Protestant and an energetic supporter of the Reformed faith in Argyll. He was at times in open rebellion against the Catholic Queen, yet in the end he became her friend and ally. Lord Argyll was Mary Queen of Scots' advisor and military commander. In fact, he was rebuked by John Knox for his easy association with Scottish Catholics. As the drama of Mary's life played out in 1567, Lord Argyll was drawn into the dramatic end of her reign as queen of Scotland. On 13 May 1568, Lord Argyll led the army in support of Mary Queen of Scots at the battle of Langside. The battle was a disaster for the Queen. Lord Argyll was ill, reportedly with an epileptic fit, and he was unable to be on the field that day when his military skills and, perhaps more importantly, his Highland Redshanks were most needed. Some of his peers say his fit was feigned and he chose not to participate in the battle on behalf of Mary. It was a mysterious and odd affair in his life, but, for whatever reason, he was not on the field that day. Mary's army was demoralized by Lord Argyll's absence and collapsed totally. His absence also prevented him from taking Mary to a place of safety in Scotland after the fiasco. She made an unwise decision to flee to England, which did allow Lord Argyll to turn his full attention back to Ulster.

The English tried to prevent the weddings of Anna and Fionnuala from taking place. The mere suggestion of the great clans of the north, O'Neill, O'Donnell, MacDonald, and Campbell, working in unison, was their worst nightmare come true. But, there was very little the English could do to prevent the event. Fitzwilliam, the English governor, warned that Tarlach Ó Neill and Aodh Ó Dónaill wanted Scottish wives in order "to breed a new sort of rebel out of their loins."[62] With great preparation, the joint weddings took place in late summer of 1569 on the island of Rathlin off the north Antrim coast. Anna and her daughter left Argyll for Islay and from there journeyed south to Rathlin. Their party included 32 galleys and around 4,000 Redshanks. The wedding celebration lasted for two full weeks and the gentry of the northern Gaelic world were in attendance.

Anna and Fionnuala played a leading role in Irish resistance to English rule in the latter half of the 1500s. They were responsible for raising Scottish support for the Irish lords they married. They were Gaelic nobility, highly educated, and up to the task. Both women had also married much older men and became, in time, de facto leaders of their husbands' clans. They controlled the flow of Redshanks into Ulster through their Campbell connections and this made them powerful and dangerous to the English.

---

[62] Dawson, *Politics*, 162.

Lord Argyll provided me with an explanation behind the Teoc McCains oral history connecting them to Mary Queen of Scots and leaving Scotland after her downfall. Lord Argyll did draw his soldiers and captains from his lands in mid-Argyll and the descendants of Duncan Roy McCain were certainly among these men. Anna Caimbeul and her daughter Fionnuala led thousands of Campbell Redshanks from mid-Argyll to Ireland after Mary Queen of Scots' downfall. The marriage of Fionnuala Nic Dhónaill, or as she is better known, Iníon Dubh, to Aodh Mac Manus Ó Dónaill in 1569 was the reason the McCains migrated from Kilmichael Glassary to Donegal.

Iníon Dubh

The River Foyle is a large, brown water, tidal river, that flows north into Loch Foyle and then on into the Atlantic Ocean. It begins at the town of Lifford in Donegal from the confluence of the Finn and Mourne rivers. The Foyle is one of the best salmon fishing areas in Ireland. The low lands on the west side of the river are called the Lagan,[63] taking that name from the Gaelic word *lagan*, meaning a hollow or low lying area. In the Lagan, on the banks of the river, is the small market town of St Johnston. The lands around St Johnston are green and fertile and there you will see the many shades of Irish green. It is a beautiful area where farms still flourish and time is marked by the changing seasons. In Elizabethan times, this part of the Lagan was called the Portlough precinct. After her marriage to Aodh Mac Manus Ó Dónaill, Iníon Dubh settled just south of St Johnston at Mongavlin castle. This is also where the McCains first appear in Ireland.

It was a highly strategic area. Not only was it fertile, rich land, but the Foyle River on the Lagan's eastern border provided easy access into O'Donnell lands. Troops were

---

[63] See Lagan map page 2.

needed there to protect the Foyle river ports. Large number of Redshanks accompanied Iníon Dubh to her new home there to accomplish this task. Accounts vary, but the number of Redshanks was certainly over 1,000. There was, throughout her time in the Lagan, an ebb and flow of Redshanks as the military needs of Clan O'Donnell dictated. Iníon Dubh was aggressive in her efforts to defend west Ulster from English rule and her weapon of choice were the tall, fair, broad shouldered Gaels of Argyll.

Iníon Dubh was a traditional Gaelic woman, but she was also able to interact with the Elizabethan English on their terms. She spent her teenage years in the Scottish court and understood the subtle nuances of politics and war. She had command of a large force of Redshanks and was not afraid to put them into use. Lughaidh Ó Cléirigh, her contemporary and biographer of her son, wrote of her "she was the head of advice and counsel of the Cenél Conaill (Clan O'Donnell), and though she was calm and very deliberate and much praised for her womanly qualities, she had the heart of a hero and the mind of a soldier,"[64] She has a unique place in Irish history. She was a Scottish aristocrat, her father the head of Clan Donald and her mother the daughter of the Campbell chief, but she became a heroine of the Irish in the north. Iníon Dubh is best remembered for her defense of her sons, who had glorious but tragic lives as Gaelic warriors.

Iníon Dubh's main residence in the Lagan was the castle at Mongavlin. She had a secondary house at Carrigans, just north of St Johnston. These locations were not random.

---

[64] Lughaidh Ó Cléirigh, *Beatha Aodha Ruaidh Uí Dhómhnaill*, trans. Paul Walsh (Cork: University College, 2012. http://www.ucc.ie/celt, 39.

Both were river harbors where the Redshank galleys could easily land. It is not a large area. Carrigans is only one and three quarters miles north of St Johnston and Mongavlin is only two and a quarter miles to its south. The Redshanks of Iníon Dubh settled around her within the five or so miles between Mongavlin and Carrigans.

The Elizabethan English were very cognizant of the Redshanks in Ireland. The *Calendar of the State Papers Relating To Ireland* has correspondences of English officials in Ulster reporting their movements from the mid-1500s onward. The English feared the Redshanks and the actions of Iníon Dubh in particular. Scotland was still considered a threat to England and so many Scots in Ireland was considered an invasion of English ruled land. Iníon Dubh used her Campbell clan connections to great effect and made many trips to Argyll to visit the fifth Earl of Argyll and his successor. She would stay for several months, recruiting her Redshanks, and return with a fleet of Gaelic galleys to her lands on the shores of the River Foyle.

There is a description of these Redshanks found in the early 1600s book *Beatha Aodha Ruaidh Uí Dhomhnaill* (Life of Aodh Rua Ó Dónaill), written by the seanchaí (historian) of Clan O'Donnell, Lughaidh Ó Cléirigh:

> They were recognized among the Irish soldier
> by the distinction of their arms and clothing,
> their habits and language, for their exterior
> dress was mottled cloaks of many colors with a
> fringe to their shins and calves, their belts were
> over their loins outside their cloaks. Many of
> them had swords with hafts of horn, large and

warlike, over their shoulders. It was necessary for the soldier to grip the very haft of his sword with both hands when he would strike a blow with it. Others of them had bows of carved woods strong for use, with well-seasoned strings of hemp, and arrows sharp pointed, whizzing in flight.[65]

Ó Cléirigh's comments referred to the arrival in Derry of a thousand Redshanks under Dónall Gorm Mac Dónaill of Skye and Mac Leóid of Arran in 1594. They were in the service of Iníon Dubh's son and part of his troop build-up at the beginning of the Nine Year's War. Ó Cléirigh was an eyewitness to these events and his account provides insight into the physical appearance of the Redshanks in the 1590s. For centuries Irish and Scottish Gaels had dressed identically in a saffron colored *léine* (long shirt to the knees) and jacket. By the late 1500s, the unique dress of the Scottish Gaels had developed and the belted kilt was worn by many Redshanks. The two handed swords and bows described by Ó Cléirigh were the favorite weapons of the Redshanks and they were proficient in their use. Ó Cléirigh also noted the dialect differences in the Gaelic spoken by these Redshanks.

Both the native Irish and the English made a distinction between the older Scots in Ireland, the Gallóglaigh, and the newer Scots, the Redshanks. The native Irish called the Redshanks, *na Albanaigh*, which simply means "the Scots." The English called them Irish-Scots, Scots-Irish, or Redshanks. By the mid-1500s, some Redshanks were settling in Ulster and

---

[65] Lughaidh Ó Cléirigh, *Beatha Aodha Ruaidh Uí Dhómhnaill*, trans. Paul Walsh (Cork: University College, 2012. http://www.ucc.ie/celt, 73.

not returning back to Scotland after the campaigning season. In 1542, John Travers, the Master of the Ordnance in Ireland wrote:

> ... where as a company of Irisshe Skottes otherwise called Redshankes daily commeth into the northe parties of Irelande and purchaseth castels and piles uppon the seecoste there so as it is thought that there be at this present above the nombre of 2 or 3 thousande of them within this Realme...[66]

In April of 1571, Lord Justice William FitzWilliam wrote to the Privy Council:

> The Scots in the North build, manure the ground, and settle, as though they should never be removed.[67]

By 1580, Iníon Dubh and her Redshanks began to dominate the political and military affairs of western Ulster. She was by this time the acting head of Clan O'Donnell. Some sources say her husband, Aodh Mac Manus, was growing senile. The reasons she took the reins of leadership were probably multiple and included her husband's age, failing health, and loss of mental clarity. Iníon Dubh's early life in the Scottish court and her links to Clan Campbell and Clan Donald gave her the needed connections and experience to protect her family's position. She also had her own army, which she paid

---

[66] Hamilton, *Calendar,* 302.
[67] Ibid., 444.

and commanded personally, and her Redshanks were completely devoted to her.

There were many threats to Iníon Dubh. The children of her husband by his first wife were rivals to her own children and there was always the English to contend with. In 1587, John Perrot, the English Lord Deputy of Ireland, wanted hostages from the O'Donnells to insure that they would not aid the Spanish in their war against England. Perrot plotted to kidnap Iníon Dubh and her husband, but only their oldest son, Aodh Rua, fell into English hands. He was imprisoned in Dublin Castle. Iníon Dubh threw all her energies into freeing her son and making him the head of Clan O'Donnell. In 1588, Iníon Dubh attempted to obtain the release of Aodh Rua by rounding up some survivors of the Spanish Armada that made land fall in Donegal and presenting them to the English in Dublin as an exchange for her son. The English took the prisoners, but had them all executed and kept Aodh Rua in his dungeon cell. She then told the English she would work with the Spanish if they did not release him, again with no success.

It was decidedly unhealthy to cross Iníon Dubh in matters relating to her children. She was in a vulnerable position with her husband in failing health and her oldest son a prisoner of the English, yet she managed to hold on to power. Her husband was thought by some within Clan O'Donnell as unfit to be head of the clan. The first rival to press the issue was Aodh Mac Calbhach Ó Gallchobhair. He was a mysterious figure, perhaps an illegitimate son of Calbhach Ó Dónaill, or perhaps fostered with Calbhach's family. Whatever the case, he let it be known he could take the headship. Aodh Mac Calbhach had cooperated with the English and had been an accomplice in the infamous murder of Iníon Dubh's first cousin, Alasdair Mac Somhairle Mac Dónaill. In 1588, Aodh Mac Calbhach attempted to visit Iníon Dubh at her castle and press the issue. Iníon Dubh was not impressed. She addressed her beloved Redshanks about the need for justice and revenge upon Aodh Mac Calbhach. They attacked Aodh Mac Calbhach while he was in St Johnstown, killing him and his entire party.

Another of Iníon Dubh's rivals was her husband's son by an earlier marriage, Dónall Mac Aodh Ó Dónaill. Dónall proclaimed himself as head of Clan O'Donnell. He also underestimated Iníon Dubh. She took command of her army of Redshanks and marched out to meet Dónaill Ó Dónaill in battle. Dónall assembled a formidable host that included his factions within Clan O'Donnell, along with allied clans. The Battle of Derrylaghan took place on 14 September 1590 when the two armies met to the south of Gleann Cholm Cille near the village of Teileann. The Redshanks used their bows to stun Dónall's army and then closed with their two handed swords. Dónall's army was crushed and he, many of the Irish nobles, and 200 of their men, were killed.

Aodh Rua finally escaped Dublin Castle in 1592. Iníon Dubh persuaded her husband to abdicate and Aodh Rua became The Ó Dónaill. Iníon Dubh bought off the last rival claiming the headship of the clan, Niall Garbh Ó Dónaill, and arranged a marriage between him and her daughter Nuala.

The English tried to oust Aodh Rua, but with no success. Aodh Rua and his Redshanks won several sharp engagements against the English. Then he allied himself with Aodh Mór Ó Neill and that began the Nine Years War (1594-1603). In the conflict, Aodh Rua and Aodh Mór Ó Neill had many victories and defeated every English army sent to destroy them in Ulster. For seven years they held the English armies at bay, but both leaders knew this could not last. English pressure on the north was increasing and the Irish sought Spanish help with the war. Spain finally managed to land a small force, but in the worst possible place, on the opposite end of the country. The small Spanish force landed in County Cork and were promptly besieged by the English under Lord Mountjoy. Aodh Rua and Ó Neill had no choice, if they wanted Spanish help, but to march across Ireland to relieve the Spanish besieged there. In Ulster, the Irish victories were due to the complete support of the people and the heavily wooded and mountainous terrain which suited the Gaelic style of war. Many of the Irish victories were fought from ambush in passes and along winding roads in deep forests or from a fixed, prepared position. These were styles of warfare that favored the Gaels. It was a great gamble for Aodh Rua and Ó Neill to abandon what had served them so well, but they needed Spanish help to push the English out of Ireland. Against their better judgment, they marched across the country to Cork to assist their besieged Spanish allies. The Battle of Kinsale was fought on 3 January 1602 when the Irish army attempted to relieve the Spanish. The Irish were forced into open field battle and were utterly defeated. Aodh Rua took a ship to Spain to organize further resistance, but he died a few months later, thought to be poisoned by an English spy.

Aodh Mór Ó Neill returned to Ulster. In 1607, he also left for Spain, along with Aodh Rua's brother, Ruairi, who had become The Ó Dónaill after Aodh Rua's death. Their intention was to raise money and an army to continue the war. They set sail from Rathmullan, a small village on the shore of Loch

Swilly in County Donegal, with ninety followers, many of them the cream of Ulster's Gaelic nobles, an event known as the Flight of the Earls. Their destination was Spain, but they landed first in France. Some made their way to Spanish Flanders, while others continued on to Rome. Their plans came ultimately to nothing and both Ruairi Ó Dónaill and Aodh Mór Ó Neill died in exile.

One of Iníon Dubh's last recorded acts was a small piece of unfinished business. Niall Garbh Ó Dónaill had turned traitor in the end, supporting the English against Aodh Rua. Iníon Dubh implicated Niall Gabh in a failed uprising in 1608 and he spent the rest of his days in the Tower of London where he died. Iníon Dubh's daughter, Nuala, left Niall Garbh, taking their children with her.

The year of 1609 brought great change in Ulster. The old Gaelic order had finally been broken and this allowed for the Plantation of Ulster. The lands of Clan O'Donnell were confiscated under James I. This included Iníon Dubh's lands at Portlough precinct in the Lagan. This part of the Lagan was planted by Scots. The two main families of Undertakers in the Portlough precinct were the Stewarts of Lennox and Cunninghams of Ayrshire. Both families had close ties to James I and received large grants of land. However, there was already a Scottish community in the Lagan. Iníon Dubh's Campbell Redshanks, including the McCains, were already living in the Portlough precinct.

Portlough Precinct

The year the McCains left Argyll for Ireland is not known. Their trail grows understandably faint from the late 1500s until they show up in records in the Portlough precinct, Donegal, Ireland, in 1630. But, their story is not hard to deduce when the history of the area is studied. The Portlough precinct was an administrative district that corresponds to Taughboyne, All Saints, Raymoghy, and part of Raphoe parishes today. Portlough precinct was the heart of the Lagan district. The McCains first appear in written records in the Portlough precinct on lands that had belonged to Iníon Dubh. The McCains were Redshanks and connected to the Earls of Argyll who settled the Redshanks in Portlough precinct and it is no surprise to find them there. Their story is found in the fate of Iníon Dubh's Redshanks after the collapse of Gaelic ruled Ulster.

By 1609, the Redshanks of Portlough precinct were no longer employed by Iníon Dubh and their ties to Clan O'Donnell were a thing of the past. There was a new order that would decide their fate. This new order was the Scottish lords that took over the O'Donnell lands in Portlough precinct. Like the O'Donnell chiefs before them, these Scottish lords valued the Redshanks for their martial abilities. Even before the Gaelic military collapse after Kinsale in the winter of 1602, the Redshank community was seen as a possible asset to British, and specifically to Scottish, interests in Ulster. This was during the end phase of the Nine Year's War at a time when the Elizabethan English were hard pressed in Ulster. British officials suggested a plan to hire the Portlough precinct Redshanks.

It was a bold idea since those Redshanks had defeated British armies on the field of battle many times in Ulster. There was naturally a concern about the loyalties of the Redshanks, but there were mitigating factors. These factors were the Redshanks' Scottish clan ties and links to important Scottish families, such as the Campbells and the Hamiltons of Arran. Iníon Dubh's mother, Anna Caimbeul, was the daughter of the third Earl of Argyll, and her cousins were the fifth and sixth Earls of Argyll. The mother of the fifth Earl of Argyll was Helen Hamilton, the eldest daughter of the first Earl of Arran, James Hamilton. Most of the Portlough precinct Redshanks were from the Campbell lands in mid Argyll or from their allies and they had a degree of loyalty to Campbell interests.

In the *Calendar of the State Papers Relating To Ireland, Of The Reign of Elizabeth*, there is correspondence promoting the use of the Portlough Redshanks. In November of 1600, the English Privy Council wrote to Henry Docwra, the English Commander in the Foyle area, suggesting the use of Redshanks. In the end, the plan was not carried out because the Irish defeat at Kinsale ended the need for the Redshanks. However, the idea of using the Foyle Redshanks was also in the minds of several prominent Scots with ambitions in Ulster. One was a kinsman of Iníon Dubh, Donnchadh Caimbeul, who was the illegitimate son of Giolla Easpuig Donn Caimbeul, the fifth Earl of Argyll. Donnchadh Caimbeul was true to his surname. Being a son of the Argyll court, he was a traditional Gael, yet he was also part of the emerging British world. Like many Campbells, he knew how to combine both the Gaelic and British political tools at his disposal to further the interest of his family, which at that point in time was shifting from the Gaelic world to promoting the interest of James VI of Scotland.

In March of 1601, Donnchadh Caimbeul wrote to Sir Robert Cecil, the English Secretary of State, suggesting the use of certain Redshanks to further British interest in Ulster. His letter is of great interest because it demonstrates how the Portlough Redshanks were viewed by the Scottish officials that would later be part of the Plantation in that area. In his letter to Cecil, Caimbeul specifies use of the "civil Irish Scots" to secure strategic areas along the Foyle River.[68] He does not mince words in his recommendations and further clarifies which Redshanks are to be used, "As for the civil Irish, the Campbells only are to be chosen." His use of the word *Irish* to describe the Campbell Redshanks was common in the English of that period since *Irish* was a synonym for *Gael* and applied to both Irish and Scottish Gaels.

Donnchadh believed the Campbell Redshanks could be counted on. Their loyalties could be assured by their Gaelic clan affiliation, and of significance, the Campbell Redshanks were Protestant. The fifth Earl of Argyll was an early convert

---

[68] Hamilton, *Calendar,* 255, 256.

to the Reformed faith and had vigorously set about converting the Campbell rank and file and their allies in mid Argyll to his new religion. It was from this population of Gaels that Iníon Dubh's Redshanks were recruited.

Donnchadh Caimbeul and Iníon Dubh were contemporaries. They would have known each other and shared a hearth fire in Inveraray castle during Iníon Dubh's trips to Argyll. Like many other well born Campbells, Donnchadh Caimbeul obtained a good position in life, in his case, as a church official in Ireland. To accomplish this he joined the Established Church. It may seem odd that a man from such a strong Reformed faith family would do this, but this was normal Campbell behavior. Among the Campbells, pragmatism was a virtue and the ends justified the means. Donnchadh Caimbeul did well in the Established Church and he served as Dean of Limerick and coadjutor Bishop there from 1588 to 1603.

As mentioned, the plans to hire the Foyle Redshanks never were carried out since by 1603 the Nine Year's War was winding down and additional troops were not needed. The letter by Donnchadh Caimbeul, however, does show how the Campbell Redshanks were viewed by the incoming Scottish Planters that settled in Portlough precinct. In March of 1603, Queen Elizabeth I died and the Scottish King James VI ascended to the united throne of England and Scotland as James I. A few months later Donnchadh Caimbeul was appointed Bishop of Raphoe in Donegal, but died before he could be consecrated. However, his idea to incorporate the Campbell Redshanks as a method of securing the lands along the Foyle did in the end happen.

Iníon Dubh remained at Mongavlin during this time. When the Plantation was implemented by James I, she was one of the native Undertakers who were given land by the Crown. On the face of it, her grant of land by the Crown would appear to be a remarkable event given her long period of resistance to English encroachment into Ulster. Put into the context of her position within the Campbell extended kinship group, which included James I, it is understandable how she managed to weather such a tumultuous storm of change. In 1611, Iníon Dubh was given 598 acres at Kilmacrenan, west of Letterkenny, where she relocated and retired from political life. There she disappears from history, one can only hope she found some sort of peace.

By 1610, Iníon Dubh's land in the Portlough precinct was in the hands of the Stewarts and Cunninghams. It is possible that the land the Stewarts received from James I in Portlough was part of the intricate etiquette of kinship and political alliances of these prominent Scottish families. The head of this Stewart family was the Duke of Lennox, Ludovic Stewart. He had accompanied James I to England in 1603 and was a member of the Royal Household and first Gentleman of the Bedchamber. He was also a cousin to Iníon Dubh through her maternal Campbell line. The Duke and his illegitimate son, John Stewart, obtained large portions of Iníon Dubh's land and her residence at Mongavlin.

Iníon Dubh's Redshanks remained on their lands in Portlough precinct after her departure. It was their Campbell connections, Reformed faith, along with their reputation as elite fighting men, which made them not only acceptable to the incoming Stewarts, but a welcomed van guard. The Redshanks could be considered British subjects in an ecumenical Scottish sense, complete with appropriate loyalties, and a version of the Protestant faith. In the Portlough area, the incoming Planter Scots came from Ayrshire and Lennox. Lennox included lands in the Scottish Gaeltacht and parts of Ayrshire were still Gaelic speaking in the early 1600s. The Scots from these areas were familiar with Gaelic language and customs and were ethnically similar to the Campbell Redshanks.

There is evidence that after the Plantation began in 1609 little changed in the Portlough precinct. In April of 1628, in the *Calendar of State Papers for Ireland*, there is a letter from King James I concerning the state of the Stewart lands in Portlough precinct. King James complains that, "(the Stewart lands)... have not been duly planted."[69] An observation followed by a threat of an inquiry into a breach of the condition of the grant. The land had been planted in truth, but in a Scottish style, which included the pre Plantation Redshanks and settlers from Lennox and Ayrshire. Another example of the nature of the Plantation in the area is found in the *The Irish Commission of 1622*, which includes a report upon the estate of Sir John Drummond that was located on the east side of the Foyle River across from the Lagan. The Drummond estate had 2 freeholders and 31 lease holders. The report comments, "and to say truly all but four or five are redshanks who are for the most part but cottagers."[70]

The muster roll for Portlough area in 1630 provides the first opportunity to locate the Redshanks in the primary

---

[69] Hamilton, *Calendar* 1625-1632, 323.
[70] Victor Treadwell, ed., *The Irish Commission 1622*, 572. Transcript of letter sent to the author by Dr William Roulston.

sources. The muster roll functions as a type of census since all the able bodied men from each household were expected to appear at the muster. By 1630, some of the original Planters had passed away, but members of the Stewart and Cunningham families still held the Portlough precinct. Despite the haphazard anglicized forms of many of the Gaelic surnames, well over half of the muster roll was of Redshank origin. There are twenty-three Campbells and a host of other surnames connected to the Campbells as allied families, such as Crawford, McAllan, McArthur, McClean, and McCain. Iníon Dubh's Redshanks and their descendants were still living on their lands in 1630.

The enduring oral history of the McKeens in New England was that *William McKean the soldier* was one of our early ancestors in Ulster. In theory, he should be present on the 1630 muster roll. I searched for him there and found him. Among the men that reported for muster on the lands of John Stewart at Mongavlin castle was *Illime McKaine*, a swordsman. *Illime* is a phonetic spelling of the Gaelic name Uilleam, or in English *William*. Several other McCain men appear in the Portlough muster rolls, but this William McKean the Soldier was remembered by name by the McCains that migrated to the New World. With the finding of William McKean the Soldier, another piece of McCain family lore fell into place and McCains still live near Mongavlin, within minutes of where Illime McKaine stood on the grounds of the castle in 1630.

The McCains and other Redshanks in the Lagan played a prominent part in the creation of the Ulster Scots community. Many Redshanks, including several McCains from the Mongavlin area, appear in the 1642 Raphoe muster roll of Sir

Robert Stewart's regiment. Sir Robert Stewart had fought with distinction in the service of King Gustavus Adolphus of Sweden and was a brilliant and well trained soldier. His regiment was part of the Lagan army that defeated the Irish under Felim Ó Neill at the battle of Glenmaquin in June 1642. The battle is often characterized as an Ulster Scots versus Irish engagement. It must be mentioned that the Irish forces on the field at Glenmaquin also had a large number of Scottish soldiers. The Irish army included the Antrim Redshanks under Dónall Gorm Mac Dónaill and additional Hebridean Redshanks led by the famous Alasdair Mac Colla.

The Lagan Army fought for over ten years in the Wars of the Three Kingdoms. They accomplished several stunning victories under Sir Robert Stewart's superb command, but eventually they had to go up against Cromwell. The conflict in Ireland was a complicated affair with the Lagan army changing sides after the Parliamentary forces executed King Charles I in January of 1649. Sir Robert Stewart was a royalist and after the king's execution he was arrested and sent to the Tower in London, but managed to escape. He returned to Ireland and resumed command of the Lagan army. He then joined forces with the Irish Confederate army and besieged Londonderry, which was held by the Parliamentarian army under Charles Coote. The siege went on for over five months and then another remarkable change of sides took place when another Irish army under Aodh Rua Ó Neill joined sides, if only temporarily, with the Parliamentarians. The Lagan army and the other Ulster Scots besieging Londonderry were not strong enough to challenge O'Neill and the Parliamentarians in battle. The siege was lifted and the Lagan army withdrew towards Connacht. Ó Neill's disruption of the coalition armies in

Ulster unwittingly prepared the way for the conquest of the province by Parliamentarian forces later in 1649. The Lagan army spent the rest of the war fighting against Cromwell's army. Some Laganeers fought on for the king under the command of Ulick de Búrca, the Earl of Clanricarde, who ironically was a Catholic. Eventually the Lagan army surrendered to Cromwell and accepted a settlement which allowed them to return in peace to their farms and families in Donegal. Knowing my own McCains were in the Lagan army and endured such a harsh defeat was humbling to me. It makes me think about what real hardships are and not complain as much.

While the Lagan Redshanks became part of the larger Ulster Scot community there, it would be wrong to assume that they lost their distinct Gaelic culture. As Dr. Peter Toner's research into the Gaeltachtaí in New Brunswick, Canada demonstrates, many of these Donegal Presbyterians remained Gaelic speaking well into the twentieth century.[71] It would have been an interesting world for them in Donegal. Many would have been bilingual in Gaelic and Lallans. Even today it is common to encounter Redshank surnames in the Donegal Gaeltacht and many of them have remained part of the traditional Gaelic community.

From the 1630s onward, the McCain story can be followed through records that survive in Ireland. The McCains in Portlough precinct thrived and soon spread to other parts of

---

[71] Dr Peter M Toner, *Confusing Identities: The Gaeltachta In New Brunswick, 1901*. The Seventeenth Biennial Ulster-American Heritage Symposium, 25-28 June 2008. Centre for Migration Studies at the Ulster American Folk Park, Omagh, N Ireland.

Donegal and across the Foyle to northwest Tyrone and later into Derry and north Antrim. Some of them that we know of are, Illime M'Kaine on the 1630 Portlough muster roll, James McKeane, John McKeane, and Thomas McKeane on the 1642 Portlough muster roll, James McKean and James McKean Jr., in the 1665 Heads and Hearth records in Taughboyne parish. Then we have the next generation of James McKeen born in 1665 and his brother John McKean born in 1667, and with them we are back where we started, at the pivotal year of 1718 and the Ulster Migration to the English Colonies.

Ulster Scots & Scots-Irish

And now to touch upon that difficult topic, the Ulster Scots, also known as the Protestant Irish, and in the New World often called the Scots-Irish. This confusing nomenclature portends the awkwardness of the subject. The McCains have both Irish and Scottish roots and they are entwined and impossible to separate. The interaction and shared history between Scotland and Ireland has been told in this book via one family, the McCains. I have been asked many times, "Are the McCains Irish or Scottish?" It is hard to answer that question simply. Ethnicity is important to many people and it is to me as well. Being from the South, I have a strong sense of Southern ethnicity, yet also after 40 years of travel in Ireland and Scotland and reconnecting with the McCain family there, I feel at home in the old country. However, there is the fundamental fact that the McCains are Highland Scots that migrated to Ireland. The McCains in Ireland today have lived there for centuries now and while they have Scottish roots they certainly are Irish as well. I often just let the Scots-Irish epithet stick to our family as somewhere in it is the truth.

The terms Ulster Scots and Scots-Irish are interchangeable to a certain extent, but I use the latter to describe the descendants of the Ulster Scots in the New World. I was born and raised in an area that was settled by and is still dominated by Scots-Irish and I know them well. My trips to Ireland and Northern Ireland brought me into modern Ulster Scots' society and I have learned about them also. During this process I noticed that the UK and Irish media often portray Ulster Scots negatively. Being a native Southerner from Mississippi, I am familiar with being a target of negative media bias. For that reason, I approached the Ulster Scot community with an open mind and assumed the negative media image was false. I was also cognizant that these were my people. Most of the branches of the McCain family in the USA and Canada are not only Ulster Scots on the paternal side but also have many maternal Ulster Scot lines. We settled in Ulster communities and married into Ulster families in both Ireland and the New World. My Grandmother McCain's maiden name was Tweedy. The Tweedys are a Lowland Scots family. Her family migrated to Ireland and settled in the 1620s. I have already commented on our connections to the Hamiltons of Tyrone and Donegal and they are at the top of the Ulster Scots' Who's Who. This marrying into one's own ethnic group was a pattern with the Scots-Irish.

Ulster Scots history is heavy with cultural and political baggage and instead of historical facts we often get politically motivated versions of their history. Ulster Scots and their Scots-Irish descendants here in the New World are a people that evoke strong feelings and opinions and they are just plain difficult to write about. As historian Kirby A. Miller put it in his *Irish Immigrants In the Lands of Canann*, "Since the early eighteenth century, Ulster Presbyterians' motives for emigration and definition and political implications of their ethnic identities in both Ireland and America have been sharply contested issues."[72] *Sharply contested issues* is an understatement as the study of Ulster Scots is akin to juggling porcupines. No matter what you write about them, some faction will take exception and call you out, that is certain.

The entire story of the Ulster Scots is not often told. Recent history books, such as James Webb's *Born Fighting, How the Scots-Irish Shaped America*, while an excellent read, gives a somewhat narrow presentation of the Ulster Scots. "Official" historian treatments, such as David Hackett Fisher's *Albion's Seed*, are bizarrely Anglocentric. Fisher's book gives the best description of northern British society I have ever read. He uses the term "Borderers" to describe the people from the western Scottish Highlands south to northern England, including those that migrated to Ulster, seemingly oblivious of Scottish Lowland and Argyll history prior to 1609. Fisher emphasizes his point by including jabs at other historians that acknowledge Scotland's Celtic origins. To many historians, the Ulster Scots sprang from the head of Zeus, like Athena, fully grown with weapons in hand at the beginning of the Plantation of Ulster. Their real history developed over many centuries and continued to do so after the Plantation began in 1609.

The stereotypical presentation of the Ulster Scots is they are Lowland Scots that settled in northern Ireland during the Ulster Plantation in the seventeenth century. That is a major part of their story, but there are more chapters to their

---

[72] Miller, *Immigrants,* 435.

history and nuances that went into their making. Some early Ulster Scot writers realized this. Students of Ulster history are familiar with the works of Rev. George Hill, a County Antrim Presbyterian minister and historian, active from the mid to late 1800s. He was writing in a politically sensitive time when Irish republicanism was on the rise, but even he felt the need to comment on some of the irony he saw in his own community. Rev. Hill observed:

> Is it not a curious and very suggestive fact that some of our most determined Protestants now in many districts of Ulster are descended from ancestors who were just as determined Roman Catholics in 1641? And, is it not an equally curious and suggestive fact that many Roman Catholics of the present day are descended maternally at least, from Protestants who suffered in 1641? [73]

Hill wrote this because many native Irish converted to the Reformed faith or the Church of Ireland in the late 1600s and early 1700s and, by his day, their descendants were part of the Ulster Scot community. The reverse happened as well, with Ulster Scots marrying into Catholic families and their children raised in that faith. In the Portlough precinct for example, some of the Cunninghams, one of the leading Planter families from Ayrshire, converted to Catholicism. Using the McCains as another example (safer that way), we were overwhelmingly Presbyterian in the 1600s, yet today there are several Roman

---

[73] Rev George Hill, *The Stewarts of Ballintoy* (Louisville: J. Adger Stewart Publications, 1900), 10-1.

Catholic branches of the family in Scotland and even more in the United States. So, even concerning religion, the story is more complex than commonly presented.

The Ulster Scots are not a monolithic slab of stone with exact dimensions and a creation date. They are a people with some diversity within their group. There are Ulster Scots that have been in Ireland since the 1500s and others that came in the early 1600s, and still others that arrived in Ireland in the late 1600s or early 1700s. The more recent arrivals might have a different sense of ethnicity than Scots that had been living in Ireland for a century or more. Ulster Scots that immigrated to the Colonies in the early 1700s also had a different sense of ethnicity than Ulster Scots that left Ireland in the 1800s. Yet, they are all Ulster Scots.

The McCains were part of a Gaelic society indigenous to both Scotland and Ireland. They lived in central Scotland for a long time, perhaps millenniums, and their home in Argyll was the heart of the Highlands. Their migration to Ireland was part of a natural flow of Gaelic people in the late 1500s. The McCains were part of the Ulster Scot ethnic group from the early 1600s onwards. They became part of an Ulster Scot zeitgeist of that age that included the Reformed faith, new political concepts, and creation of a new order in Ulster. The McCains served in the Lagan army in the 1640s and they really did participate in the defense of Derry in the 1689 siege.[74, 75] James McKeen was a co-leader of the epic 1718 fleet that began the Ulster Migration and was a founder of the Londonderry, New Hampshire settlement. So, the McCain

---

[74] *Portlough Precinct Muster Rolls 1630, Raphoe Muster Rolls 1642.*
[75] Miller, *Immigrants,* 437.

Ulster Scot credentials are bona fide, and yet they are Gaels from Argyll, not Lowland settlers. The McCain story is not an anomaly. Many Ulster Scot families have Highland Scottish ancestry, which is another aspect of the group often ignored.

Scots have been part of Ireland and especially part of Ulster since before there was a recognizable Scottish nation. Both Lowland and Highland Scots were active in and migrating to Ulster throughout its history. Even if we restrict the discussion to medieval times and beyond, this shared history is particularly rich. It was the Ó Neill and other kings and lords in the north of Ireland that declared the Scottish Edward Bruce of Ayrshire high king of Ireland in 1316 AD. His campaign in Ireland to secure this kingship is commonly portrayed as an invasion, but it was not, as he was accepted as high king by the Irish in Ulster. Edward Bruce was the younger brother of the king of Scotland, Robert Bruce, and the Bruce family made their claim to kingship of both Ireland and Scotland by right of their Gaelic blood on their maternal side.[76] Edward's mother, Marjorie, Countess of Carrick, was an Ayrshire Gael. In the 1300s, most of the west Lowlands of Scotland were still part of the Gaelic world. Marjorie's grandfather, Cailean, married the daughter of Niall Rua, a lord in Tír Eogháin in Ulster. Edward Bruce had been fostered in Ireland and if he spoke Norman French to his father it should also be remembered that Gaelic was his mother tongue. Edward Bruce is just one chapter in Ulster Scot history. This history continues on through the movement of the Scottish Gallóglaigh clans to Ulster in the 1300s and beyond, through

---

[76] Sir James Fergusson, trans., *Declaration of Arbroath* (National Archives of Scotland, 2009).

the many marriages between the prominent houses of Ulster and Scotland, through the movement of the Redshanks into Ulster in the 1500s, and of course, the great migration of Lowland Scots to Ulster during the Plantation. The Ulster Scots are better understood when their entire history is considered.

The McCains began to leave Ireland well before there was a Northern Ireland and well before the creation of the Orange Order in 1796. We began our migration to the American Colonies in 1718 and most of the subsequent waves of the family had arrived in the New World before 1800. Like many other Ulster Scot families that migrated in the 1700s, the descendants of these earlier settlers have no sense of sectarianism as practiced in modern Northern Ireland. The McCains had been gone for generations, over a century, when these issues began to grow in importance in a modern context. The McCains and their ilk had evolved into the Scots-Irish on the American frontier and hinterlands and had more pressing issues facing them.

Scots-Irish in Colonial America formed Hibernia societies and often described their ethnicity as simply Irish. The term Scots-Irish, or more commonly put, Scotch-Irish, was often used by outsiders to describe and differentiate them from Catholic Irish. By the mid-1700s, Ulster Presbyterian merchants and professionals in Boston, New York, Philadelphia, and other east coast cities, joined with Anglican and even Catholic Irish, in celebrating St Patrick's Day and organizing specifically Irish societies and associations. Thomas McKean, a signer of the Declaration of Independence and prominent Irish Presbyterian, served as president of the

Hibernian Society for the Relief of Emigrants from Ireland in Philadelphia in 1790.[77] The Ulster Scot Diaspora, at least that part of it that migrated before the early 1800s, carried with them a sense of Irishness in a broad ecumenical manner as do many of their descendants today, yet at the same time there has always been acknowledgment of and pride in their Scottish roots.

Religious affiliation is very important in contemporary Ulster Scot society; that Protestant versus Catholic thing. However, on this side of the water, religion gradually ceased to be a defining precept of Ulster Scots. As the Ulster Scots peopled the Colonial frontier, they lost their Presbyterian faith in many cases. The Presbyterian faith in Colonial American suffered the same fate as did the Catholic faith in the Lowlands of Scotland centuries before. The hierarchical organization of the Reformed faith was urban in its outlook and did not work well on the frontier. There were a lack of trained pastors and the infrastructure collapsed. Many Scots-Irish went from Presbyterian to Methodist or Baptist and variations upon those faiths. In the American Old South West and Southwest, there were some Scots-Irish families that became Catholic due to Spanish and French influences there. This is not to say that the Presbyterian faith was not a defining factor of the Scots-Irish psyche. In fact, I think it was. There is a profound element in the Ulster Scot to Scots-Irish cultural continuum and I like to call it the Calvinistic code. This code is a belief system that lived beyond its Presbyterian roots and was carried into the

---

[77] DNA testing proved Thomas McKean's family is not related my McCain family. He is however the same McCain family as the famous Southern ante bellum Methodist theologian, Alexander McCaine, which has links to County Cavan, Ireland.

new faiths adopted by the Scots-Irish. It is an identifiable cultural trait of the Scots-Irish to this day. The code is one of fierce independence and self-reliance, the ability to shun idle contemplation, and strive against all comers, be they men or nature, and to not only endure, but prevail.

It is not only the Scots-Irish in the New World that have travelled beyond past cultural norms. The same thing has happened to the Ulster Scots that remained home in Ireland. One interesting aspect about the contemporary Ulster Scot community in the six counties is the adoption of Highland Gaelic cultural icons as their own. I see this phenomenon as a natural, organic process, and as a growing awareness of their Celtic roots. It is ironic, none the less, because in the 1600s most Highland Scots were Catholic and sided with the Papal forces in the wars of the Three Kingdoms and did so again in the Williamite War.

In Ulster, the Irish opposition to the Plantation settlers came in large part from Highland Scots led by the MacDonalds of Antrim. In the 1640s, the Irish army that fought against the Presbyterian Scots in Ulster included many Antrim Redshanks and other Scottish Gaels led by Alasdair Mac Colla. In the Williamite War on 7 December 1688, when the thirteen Apprentice Boys locked the gates of Derry to keep out the Irish army, the Irish that the doors were shut on were Scottish Redshanks from Antrim led by their chief, the Earl of Antrim, Alasdair Mac Dónaill. The bulk of his *Irish* troops were Scots, wearing kilts, playing bagpipes, speaking Gaelic, with papal flags and priests in their entourage. And yet, today Presbyterian Ulster Scots play the pipes and wear kilts in their annual parades and celebration. It is an interesting conflation.

Another aspect of Ulster Scots culture that I find fascinating is the borrowing of American Southern music. There are dozens of very good Ulster Scot Bluegrass and Old Time bands in Ireland and Northern Ireland today. The Ulster Scot community has reached out to their Diaspora in the American South to borrow back their Ulster music, albeit in the New World Celtic hillbilly format. The reverse has also happened. Old Time and Blue Grass musicians in the South have borrowed music styles, instruments, and repertoire, from Ireland and their music has evolved from the exchange. Some academics howl at this process and think it artificial, but it is not. It is organic. It is just the normal cultural flow between homeland and Diaspora. It is a sign that the Ulster Scots and their Scots-Irish kinsfolk have a resilient society and culture with a future before them.

Language is another interesting aspect of the Ulster Scots. Ulster Scots have two native languages, Gaelic and Lallans. The former has fallen out of favor with many Ulster Scots because Gaelic now has a perceived political association with Irish republicanism. However, in the real world, the Ulster Scots played a crucial role in helping the Gaelic language to survive into the twenty-first century. There were significant numbers of Gaelic speaking Ulster Scots in Donegal, Tyrone, and north Antrim. Gaelic speaking Ulster Scots took their language with them when they migrated to the New World. Canadian historian Professor Peter Toner Sr., in his examination of Canadian census records, proved that the Irish language was spoken in New Brunswick from the mid-1800s well in to the twentieth century. The interesting fact revealed by Dr. Toner's research was that the language was preserved not by Irish Catholics, but by Protestant Irish from west Ulster, primarily, Donegal and Tyrone. The denial of Gaelic origins by so many Irish Protestants he calls "The Great Amnesia." Even in my own research of my McCains, I found sources that mention the use of Gaelic in the Scots-Irish communities, not only in Colonial times but even into the mid-1800s.

As mentioned in an earlier chapter, literally the first book published in Gaelic was done by the Reformed faith Bishop Seon Carsuel. His family was from Wigtown in Gallowayshire in the Scottish Lowlands, which was still Gaelic speaking in the 1500s. His preface in the book gives insight into his world and the world of the McCains (quote left in Carsuel's dialect and syntax with spellings modernized):

> Is mór an leatrom agus an uireasa atá riamh orainne Gaeil Alban agus Éireann, thar a chuid eile den domhain, gan ár gcanúint Gaeilge a chur i gcló riamh, mar atá á gcanúint agus a dteanga féin i gcló ag gach uile chineál dhaoine eile sa domhain... (sic) (We Scottish and Irish Gaels have suffered great distress and deficiency more than other parts of the world because our language has not been printed, in contrast to other countries...)[78]

That was written by a Scottish Lowlander and reveals a historical reality that has been forgotten by many. What is of interest to me about this is, when Seon Carsuel wrote that in 1567, he lived at Carnasserie castle in mid Argyll within a

---

[78] Roger Blaney, *Presbyterians and the Irish Language* (Belfast, Ulster Historical Foundation 1996), 162-163.

couple miles of the McCains in Dunamuck. He saw the smoke from the McCain hearth fires from his window.

Irish Protestants continued their support of Gaelic language in the published word. In 1631, they published Calvin's Catechism and by 1710 they had published the Bible, *Confession of Faith,* and Presbyterian Catechism, all in literary Irish. In the late 1700s and 1800s, most of the dynamic work being done to promote Gaelic language in Ireland was done by Presbyterians. In the 1830s, Belfast was the first place in Ireland to have a society devoted to promoting the Irish language. The first dictionary of Irish was compiled in Belfast. It was Irish Presbyterians that took the lead in these projects. At the time when Ulster Protestants were supporting the Gaelic language, the Irish nationalist, Daniel O'Connell, did the opposite. Despite being a native Gaelic speaker, he thought Gaelic to be a hindrance to his nationalist cause and recommended that the Irish embrace English.

In bringing these facts to light, I am in no way trying to diminish the importance of Lallans. Lallans is part of the Ulster Scot identity and I wish it to flourish. Some of our McCain relatives in Ireland still speak Lallans. What I am saying is that Ulster Scots also have another language, which is Gaelic, and there was historically a significant Gaelic speaking Ulster Scots population. The Presbyterian Irish support for Gaelic has not entirely disappeared and a growing number of Ulster Scots remain active in the Irish speaking community in Ulster today. Also of interest, Gaelic language learning in the Diaspora is a growing phenomenon and attracts many Scots-Irish students.

In the past, some American Scots-Irish had a better understanding of their roots than is common today. An example of this can be seen in *The Scotch-Irish In America,* which is a book of the proceedings of the Scotch-Irish Congress at Columba, Tennessee, May 1889. One of the main speakers was Rev. D. C. Kelley and his talk mentions the Redshank movement into Ulster in the 1500s, a major event that is rarely included in modern Scots-Irish histories. The Scotch-Irish Congress in 1889 also welcomed men of all faiths, including Roman Catholic, a practicality given the religious diversity in the Scots-Irish community by the 1880s.

Some champions of the Scots-Irish in the late 1800s and early 1900s had a more narrow view than was evident at the 1889 Congress, however. There were writers that denied any cultural or ethnic connections or similarities between the Scots-Irish and the Irish or Scottish Highlanders. In 1906, Scots-Irish historian John Walker Dinsmore wrote;

> Whatever blood may be in the veins of the genuine Scotch-Irishman, one thing is certain and that is there is not mingled with it one drop of the blood of the old Irish or Kelt. … if you run down the Highland Scot and the Old Irish to their deepest root, you will come to a common taproot in the ancient Celt or Kelt... The Lowland Scotch, however, were a quite different stock. They were of Teutonic or Anglo-Saxon origin, and were separated from

their neighbors on either side by race, language, religions and personal traits.[79]

It would be hard to be more wrong than J. W. Dinsmore. Not only is their blood mingled, but it is the same blood, or better said, the same DNA. The people of the Scottish Lowlands have the same DNA haplogroups as the native Irish in Ulster and the Highland Scots. The most common of these DNA haplogroups is called the Northwest Irish modal, but recent research has shown it is also so prevalent in the Scottish Lowlands that many researchers have renamed this haplogroup as the *Northwest Irish and Lowlands Modal*. In geneticist speak, it is the R-M222 branch defined by a single nucleotide polymorphism called M222. In the vernacular, they are the same bunch of Celts. The history of the Lowlands is one of Celtic kingdoms, some which survived well into medieval times. Both Cumbric and Gaelic are the ancestral languages of the Lowlands and there were still Gaelic speaking areas in the western Lowlands when the Ulster Plantation began. For a long time, however, Mr. Dinsmore's ideas were often repeated and one can still hear them from time to time. What emerged was the idea of Ulster Scots as some sort of half-caste Anglo-Saxon. Good enough to fight and build an Empire, but not quite up to Home County or Eastern Establishment standards of breeding or manners.

The adoration of King William and the crown in general is another interesting aspect of contemporary Ulster Scots when compared to their Scots-Irish kinsmen in the New

---

[79] John Walker Dinsmore, *The Scotch-Irish in American: Their History, Traits, Institutions, and Influences* (Chicago: Winona Publishing Company , 1906), 7-8.

World. King William did secure victory for the Protestant Irish, but he was indifferent to Presbyterians in Ireland in the late 1600s and early 1700s. He was the leader of Protestant Britain, but he was also a politician and was friends with the Pope and had Catholics in high positions in both his army and court. In 1704, shortly after his death, a law was passed requiring anyone holding public office to produce a certificate stating they had received communion in the Established Church. Twenty-four Presbyterian members of the Londonderry Corporation resigned rather than submit to this procedure. In 1707, under his successor, Queen Anne, Presbyterians were subject to the infamous Penal Laws. The Toleration Act of 1719 did grant the freedom of worship for Presbyterians in Ireland, but the resentment toward the Anglican Church and the anglicized Protestant Ascendancy remained and was a contributing factor in the massive migration of Ulster Scots to the English Colonies. In my research on the McCain family, I located one letter that gave me insight into the politics of the family at the time we left Ireland. One Arkansas McCain branch wrote in 1925 the views of their early 1700s McCain immigrants as remembered by their own grandparents, "Our family left Ireland after the siege Londonderry, as they felt very bitter against England."[80] This sentiment came from Ulster Scot Presbyterians that had defended Londonderry during the 1689 siege.

Many Scots-Irish were supporters of independence from Britain in the 1770s and they provided more than their share of soldiers to fight the British. The Scots-Irish in the

---

[80] William D McCain, *Seven Generations of Alexander Hamilton McCain (1786-1838) and His Wife* (Hattiesburg, MS: 1973), 24.

Carolinas, Pennsylvania, and Virginia were particularly active in the Revolution. Captain Johann Heinricks of the Hessian Jäger Corps in the British army wrote in a letter dated 18 January 1778, "Call this war by whatever name you may, only call it not an American rebellion; it is nothing more or less than a Irish-Scotch Presbyterian rebellion."[81] The quote is so apropos that many historians have thought it just lore making and was not really written, but it was, and it does sum up the attitude of many Scots-Irish toward Britain at that time. The Scots-Irish in Mecklenburg County, North Carolina, declared their independence from Britain on 20 May 1775 in the Mecklenburg Declaration, over a year before the Declaration of Independence was signed. Of course, Scots-Irish support of the war against Britain was not universal, especially in the early years of the war. There were some Scots-Irish who were part time patriots at best and were very uncomfortable siding with tidewater Planters. However, as the war progressed and men died and farms were burned, resentment against Britain grew within the Scots-Irish communities.

This anti-British mind set was reinforced when Britain armed Indian tribes during the War of 1812. This led to a brutal war between the Scots-Irish and Red Stick Creek Indians in the Deep South. There were many hundreds of Scots-Irish murdered in the opening stages of the conflict. On 30 August 1813, some 517 men, women, and children were killed by Indians at the infamous Fort Mims Massacre in Alabama. Scots-Irish icon, Andrew Jackson, finally conquered the Red Sticks, but the bitterness against the British was not forgotten.

---

[81] Extracts from the Letter Book of Captain Johann Heinricks of Hessian Jäger Corps, 1778-1780, *The Pennsylvania Magazine of History and Biography, Volume 22, No 2* (1898) 137.

There were no fond memories for things British among the Scots-Irish and this lasted for many generations. The Scots-Irish lack of affinity for and cultural identity with Britain, so crucial to the modern Ulster Scot identity, never grew in the Scots-Irish communities. This fact amazes my Ulster Scot friends in Ulster when they discover this discrepancy.

The complexities and ironies of Ulster Scot and Scots-Irish people, however, do not take away from their being a people with a shared history, culture, and ethnicity. If you were to make a short list of the most dynamic tribes on the planet, the Ulster Scots/Scots-Irish are on it and they are still making an impact. The Scots-Irish in the United States still retain the values and traits of their ancestors. Politically, they are the largest voting bloc in many of the so-called Red States. They are a good people, that can be hard and hard headed, yet these traits are also responsible for their successes and accomplishments. A list of prominent Scots-Irish would be long indeed and run the gambit from Neil Armstrong to John Wayne.

Since the Good Friday Agreement in 1998, there has been a cultural awakening within the Ulster Scot community. This has led to more communication between the Ulster Scots and their Diaspora. This, in turn, has been a catalyst for many Scots-Irish to embrace their history and culture. Hopefully, it will lead to an appreciation of just how deep and rich this history really is. This renewed interest is needed because Scots-Irish have a muddled history. Historian Patrick Griffin titled his 2001 history of the Scots-Irish *The People With No Name*. In my experience, they know who they are and know they are still a people. They are in many ways an indigenous people, the unhyphenated Americans.

Ultimately, the Ulster Scots and Scots-Irish have a place in the greater Celtic world. To tell their history you must start with the ancient Celtic tribes of north Britain and continue on through the beginning of Scotland in medieval times, to changes in faith and languages, to a shared experience in Ulster and on the American frontier and in the woods and rivers of New Brunswick and the other corners of the earth where they now live, and the McCains are part of that story.

Cultural Continuum

Austin Rock, a native Dubliner, provided a lot of assistance to me in finding the McCains. In retrospect, it was mostly moral support given during the dark days of the hunt prior to the DNA testing that provided the breakthrough. Austin was always there for me when I sounded out a new theory on the McCains. He was unflinching in his assistance and, being in Dublin, he often secured old documents from dusty library shelves there that allowed me to explore a new line of my research. Austin eventually created a Rock family DNA project and successfully recovered the history of his own family, finding dozens of cousins through his DNA results. I have travelled in Ireland for four decades now and I learned a lot about real Ireland through my friendship with Austin. For me, there is a relationship between homeland and Diaspora that I see as a cultural continuum.

Austin lives in north Dublin and I have stayed at his house during my trips to Ireland. From his attic bedroom, I could look out across Dublin to the Wicklow Mountains to the south. It is a post card view of the old Baile Átha Cliath.

Austin has taken me to his favorite places in Dublin and out into the counties around the city. We have spent hours and hours visiting Tara Hill and many of the archaeological sites in the Boyne valley. My first meeting with Austin was in the fall of 2000 during the same trip that took me to Northern Ireland.

Loughcrew in County Meath is Austin's favorite place to visit. For years he had sent me email reports of his weekend visits to Loughcrew and these included accounts of bizarre occurrences up on top of Sliabh na Caillí, which is the main hill at the site. Sometimes he would be up there and a feeling would come over him, one of sheer and utter dread, and he would know he had better leave. It seems that every time he went to the place something happened to him, odd things like raven attacks or queer winds that came from nowhere and almost blew him into the next county. He began to believe that these things were caused by the *Hag*. The Hag is the spirit that haunts Loughcrew and her abode is Sliabh na Caillí. Austin thought that for some reason she had taken a dislike to his visits, or perhaps was testing his mettle, or reminding him that it was *She* who must be respected if these visits were to continue. When Austin took me to Loughcrew, it was an interesting and spooky visit.

Austin Rock is one of those Irishmen that positively attracts magic as flowers attract bees. Ireland is still a magical place despite the dreary secular malaise that has invaded the island. One of our trips to Loughcrew is an example. It was a wet fall day the first time he took me to the Neolithic cairns at Loughcrew. It is a beautiful spot, surrounded by miles and miles of green Irish countryside. Loughcrew is a series of hills upon which there are cairns and burial passages of great age, constructed some five or six thousand years ago. The ruins there are un-restored and you see them as they exist now after so many millennia have passed by. Loughcrew has one of Ireland's four largest passage tomb cemeteries and long-forgotten kings, queens, and warriors sleep there. That alone is enough to make the hair stand up on the back of your neck, but also it has *the Hag*. Loughcrew in Gaelic is Loch na Craoibh, meaning *lake of the tree*. Sliabh na Caillí is commonly translated as *Hill of the Hag*.

On my first visit to Loughcrew with Austin, we parked the car and walked up the hill to the top where the tombs and standing stones are located. What a sight! As you look out at the vista, you see several counties of the midlands of Ireland and a landscape of green rolling hills and woods. Ravens circle above watching you and the wind is in your hair. The wind blows cold upon the hill top and it is a wonderful and mysterious place. We stayed on the hill for some time with Austin pointing out each aspect of the ancient ruins. When the time came to leave and we began our hike down the hill, Austin chanced a comment about this being the first time the Hag did not try to get him. He looked at me as he said this and, as the last word of his sentence was still on his lips, he disappeared from my sight, pop, he was gone. I gathered my wits and realized he had slipped on the wet turf and he was off like a shot down the mountain, like a supine luger going down the Cresta Run in St Moritz in Switzerland. Austin was moving like a bullet from a gun!

Sliding down a hill at high speed might seem humorous, but there was considerable danger. There are boulders and jagged rock outcroppings everywhere and poor

Austin was at their mercy. A collision with anyone of them could have popped his noggin like a nut in a cracker. I took off after him, but his speed was no match for my legs and I watched him disappear off in the green of the steep hill at a frightful pace. I ran till I was sucking Irish air in like forge bellows. Finally, I saw him collapsed down below, his body rhythmically shaking. I feared the worst, broken everything and head wounds with convulsions, but as I looked into his face I realized, no, he was laughing insanely! He looked up and said, "She got me again." And so she had. The Hag likes gestures. There was Austin bragging about how he escaped the visit without a scratch or scare and, before he could finish his sentence, she got him again. I, for one, will never call her the Hag. She will always be addressed affectionately as... the Lady.

The story does not end there, however. I helped Austin up. He had lost some flesh and some bits of material from his trousers' seat, and there was a little sheep poo here and there. Other than that, he was ok and we made it to the car and set off. It was raining of course, after all this is Ireland we are talking about. We drove and drove and Austin gave me a puzzled look. He wasn't quite sure where we were despite his being familiar with the roads. He pulled the car to the side of the road, organized his thoughts, asked me my opinion (as if a Mississippian would know the roads to and from Loughcrew), and then we set off again. We were very surprised when we pulled up to the Loughcrew parking area that we had left only twenty minutes before. We had made no turns and had gone straight, and yet, we were back where we started. We stopped, looked at each other, discussed the situation and set off again. This time the roads were familiar, as they should have been, and we managed to get home without any further gestures from the Lady.

When I returned home to Mississippi, I researched the Lady and found her story. The Lady is Cailleach Béara and she was, or perhaps still is, a luminary of the Tuatha De Danann who managed to endure into our times. Several of the old Tuatha De Danann still have a small following in parts of Ireland and Scotland. For those who do not know, Tuatha De Danann, is one of the names of the high fairies or elves, as Tolkien liked to call them. These are not your diminutive wee folk, but luminous creatures of light, tall and fair, wonderful, powerful, and dangerous to be around. Béara was a Bean Sí which means *fairy woman* and is often anglicized as *banshee*. Loughcrew is one of her fairy mounds.

Cailleach Béara is called Cally Berry in Ulster English and you will also hear her called Gentle Annie, Old Woman of the Mountains, and Caill Bhuere in Argyll. Cailleach is normally translated as the Hag or Witch, but Cailleach really means *veiled one*. The root word is Caille, meaning *veil*. The word cailleach makes its way into many Irish compound nouns. A cailleach phráta is a shrivelled potato and a cailleach oíche is an owl. A cailleach feasa is a wise woman or fortune teller and a cailleach dhubh is the term for a nun. Some remember Béara as a primordial nature spirit and Queen of Winter. She can appear as an old woman or as a beautiful young maiden that is tall and fair. Everyone with sense feared her. When angry, Béara was as fierce as the biting north wind and harsh as a gale from the sea. Each winter she reigned as Queen, but when spring drew near Béara would lose her power to Aonghus Óg,

King of Summer. She apparently still watches over Loughcrew.

The mystery of Loughcrew and my experiences there added to my understanding of the culture from which the McCain family originated. Béara is still remembered in Kilmichael Glassary where the McCains originated. The lore of the district says she created Loch Awe and stories of her were told around McCain hearths in times past when we lived there. My trip to Loughcrew connected me in a tangible way to the Gaelic world of my ancestors. Seon Carsuel, Bishop and pastor to the fifth Earl of Argyll, complained about the mid-Argyll Gaels reverence of the old ways. In particular, he cited the Tuatha De Danann. Carsuel lived in Carnasserie Castle in Kilmartin Glen just minutes from where McCains were living in the 1500s. In 1567, when the McCains were literally his neighbors, he wrote concerning the locals preference of traditional Gaelic literature:

> ...darkness of sin and ignorance and design of those who teach and write and cultivate Gaelic, that they are more designed, and more accustomed, to compose vain, seductive, lying and worldly tales about the Tuatha De Danann and the sons of Mil and the heroes and Finn MacCoul and his warriors and to cultivate and piece together much else which I will not enumerate or tell here, for the purpose of

winning for themselves the vain rewards of the world.[82]

Seon Carsuel was writing about the McCains and the other Gaelic families he had to deal with in Argyll. Carsuel described a cultural continuum that was still alive in the 1500s and yet dated to the Bronze Age. At Loughcrew, I had experienced something that would have been familiar to my McCain ancestors in Kilmichael Glassary. What would the good Bishop think if he knew centuries later at least some Gaels still enjoyed the "vain, seductive, lying and worldly tales" of the Tuatha De Danann? No offense meant to the good Bishop, but it is reassuring to know that tales of the Tuatha De Danann live still and I had been fortunate enough to participate in one.

I did find the McCains in Ireland and learn our history, which were my original goals, but that was not an end of the story. There is not a day that goes by that I do not receive at least one email from a McCain cousin that I located through our DNA Project. I am sent photos, updates of marriages and births, and sad news of passings. I am not the only McCain that travels to Ireland these days. Many others now go over and visit with our relations and enjoy the hospitality of Ireland. I hear of their trips back to Ireland and some have crossed the North Channel and have visited Kilmichael Glassary parish in Argyll. The circle of life in family and clan continues.

There were some surprises for me on the odyssey. I never expected to find primary sources that supported

---

[82] Anne Ross, *The Folklore of the Scottish Highlands* (New York: Sterling Publishing, 1993), 17.

Elizabeth Spencer's memory of the Teoc McCains' oral history. The story of our connections to Mary Queen of Scots and leaving Scotland after her downfall sounded like some romantic flourish grafted onto our story. And yet, as I pieced the history together there was quality circumstantial evidence that supported the story. The McCains were captains for the fifth Earl of Argyll and he really was Mary's military commander and one of her chief advisors. We did show up in Ireland after Mary's fall from power. Equally surprising was finding William McKean the Soldier who was remembered by the New England McKeens. I thought the man was just a myth, but there he was on the 1630 muster roll at Mongavlin where the McCains still live to this day. Discovering the McCains' origins in Argyll was also unexpected. In the end, I had a reasonably good history of the McCains, which is remarkable given the difficulty in doing research on Gaelic families prior to 1600.

The physical artifacts of McCain history are rapidly fading. The stone of Duncan Roy McCain is much more weathered today and harder to read than it was when Captain White visited it the 1870s. This is happening to the old McCain graves in Templastragh Church in County Antrim also. The transcript of the inscription of the McCain grave located there was done in the 1830s by a British Army survey team. When I visited Templastragh in 2004, I found the stone considerably more faded and difficult to read. Perhaps acid rain is hastening the weathering of these artifacts. For whatever reason, the stones and their stories are fading fast.

Time consumes even stone and they are returning to the earth. The people, the McCains sleeping under the stones, are remembered, however, and they take their place in the line of our ancestors. While I was working on this book, Wallace McCain, the Canadian food baron passed away. He sent me a letter and a book he had commissioned on his branch of the family before he passed on. That book is sitting in a stack of books on the floor by my desk right now, a reminder of him. Other McCains that I have met through the DNA test have passed away also, from illness or age. They, too, take their place in the line of our ancestors. Meeting them made my life richer. There have also been many McCain births and all is as it should be. The story continues and I feel like my duty as seanchaí was performed well.

There is still more history to discover of course. Y chromosome DNA not only locates cousins and the area where your ancestors lived in the last few centuries, it also provides a window into the distant past. In the last few years a watershed event has taken place in the field of early Western European history. It is a paradigm shift that has totally changed how early European history will be taught. It is the concept that Celtic languages and the people that spoke them originated in the Atlantic Zone during the Bronze Age and the Iberian Peninsula was the starting point. This new theory is a major departure from the long-established, but increasingly problematic paradigm from late Victorian times, in which ancient Celtic languages and people were linked to the Hallstatt and La Tene cultures of west-central Europe. This research is being carried out at the University of Wales Centre for Advanced Welsh and Celtic Studies. In 2013, Dr. John Koch, who heads the project, and archaeologist Dr. Barry Cunliffe, co-edited *Celtic From the West 2*. This book is an excellent presentation of where the field of Celtic studies stands in the first part of the twenty-first century. I see evidence of the new paradigm even in the McCain DNA results. Every month I bring up the McCain DNA matches and look at the distant match group. It is large, numbering in the thousands, and includes many matches to men in northern Portugal and northern Spain. These are our very distant McCain cousins.

I hope this memoir encourages other families to find their ancestors. Ancestors and heritage are wonderful gifts to give children. It strengthens them to know who they are and to learn about the generations of their people that made it possible for them to be here today. My two sons have a healthy interest in history. When they were boys I asked them once, "do you want to see an ancient Celt." Of course they did. I made them close their eyes and led them in front of a mirror and told them to, "look." They did and they saw the face of their ancestors. We are literally our ancestors, we carry their DNA and their blood is our blood.

Research at Emory University School of Medicine suggest that even the memories, feelings, and experiences of our ancestors are saved and held in the DNA helix. This DNA memory could be an aroma or geographic location, music, or anything that was part of your ancestors' world and deeply imprinted on them. When you experience one of these sensations, the memories of your ancestors awaken in you. I know this personally. Several times in Ireland and Scotland, when I was where McCains had lived for many hundreds of years, there were moments when I felt my ancestors awaken in me. Imagine standing where your ancestors lived for a thousand years and hearing a familiar sound of wind through trees, the smell of the turf, the look of the sky and clouds. You experience the same connections and familiarity with sight and sound and the physical attributes of a place as did your ancestors. It happens, it is in your DNA.

The McCains did not do too badly over the centuries. We were not kings or Highland chiefs, but we did have our place in society in Argyll, then in Ulster, and, when we left our homeland, we did alright in the places we settled. It was a long odyssey finding the McCains. From Oxford, Mississippi, to County Donegal, Ireland, is a great distance in both time and geography. However, I am home in both places. It is my heritage and I am looking forward to my next pint of Guinness down at Kee's Hotel in Stranorlar and enjoying the company of family and friends there.

Bibliography

Akenson, Donald Harman. *Being Had: Historians, Evidence, and the Irish in North America.* Ontario: P.D. Meany Publishers, 1985.

Bigger , Francis Joseph, and William J Fennell. "Teampull Lastrach, Dunseveric, Co Antrim," *Ulster Journal of Archaeology*, Vol. 5. Belfast: The Linenhall Press, 1899.

Broderick, George. "The Breton Movement and the German Occupation 1940-44: Alan Heusaff and Bezen Perrot: A Case-Study". PhD diss., University of Mannheim, 2005.

Burnett, George, ed. *Exchequer Rolls of Scotland*, Vol. IX. Edinburgh: H M General Register House, 1886.

Dawson, Jane E A. *The Politics of Religion in the Age of Mary Queen of Scots, The Earl of Argyll and the Struggle for Britain and Ireland.* Cambridge: Cambridge University Press, 2002.

Dawson, Jane E A. *Campbell Letters*. Edinburgh: Scottish Historical Society, 1997.

Day, Angélique, ed., Patrick McWilliams, ed., and Nóirín Dobson, ed. *Ordance Survey Memoirs of Ireland*, Vol.24. Belfast: The Institute of Irish Studies, The Queen's University of Belfast, 1994.

Dinsmore, John Walker. *The Scotch-Irish in American: Their History, Traits, Institutions, and Influences.* Chicago: Winona Publishing Company , 1906.

Drummond, James. *Sculptured Monuments in Iona & The West Highlands.* Edinburgh: Society of Antiquaries of Scotland, 1881.

Fergusson, Sir James, trans. *Declaration of Arbroath.* National Archives of Scotland, 2009.

Hamilton, Hans Claude, ed. *Calendar of the State Papers Relating to Ireland.* London: Longman, Green, Longman & Roberts, 1860.

Harwood, H W Forsyth, ed. 'Extracts from Poltalloch Writs;' *The Genealogist,* Vol. 38. London: G Bell & Sons, Ltd., 1922.

Hazard, Samuel, ed. *Pennslyvania Archives,* Vol.1. Philadelphia, 1852.

Hill, Rev George. *The Stewarts of Ballintoy.* Louisville: J. Adger Stewart Publications, 1900.

Innes, Cosmo Nelson, ed., and others. *Origines Parochiales Scotiae,* Vol. 2, Pt 1. Edinburgh: The Bannatyne Club, 1854.

James, Frances Heather, *Medieval rural settlement, a study of Mid Argyll, Scotland*, PhD thesis, University of Glasgow, 2009.

Jenkins, Howard M. ed. *Pennsylvania Colonial and Federal: A History 1608-1903,* Vol.1. Philadelphia: Pennslyvania Historical Publishing Association, 1903.

Lamont, Sir Norman, ed. *Inventory of Lamont Papers.* Edinburgh: J Skinner & Co. Ltd., 1914.

MacPhail, JRN, ed. *Highland Papers*, Vol. 2, Edinburgh, University Press, 1916.

McCahan,Robert. *M'Cahan's Local Histories*. Coleraine: Glens of Antrim Historical Society, 1988.

McCain Family DNA Project, http://mccaindna.ulsterheritage.com/.

McCain, John and Mark Salter. *Faith of My Fathers*. New York: Harper Collins Publishing, 1999.

McCain, William D. *Seven Generations of the Family of Alexander Hamilton McCain (1786-1836) and His Wife, Naomi Neely McCain (1800-1874), of North Carolina, South Carolina, Georgia, Alabama, and Mississippi*. Hattiesburg, MS: 1973.

McConnell, Dr James. Institute for Scots-Irish Studies. *The 1718 Migration*, http://www.1718migration.org.uk/s_home.asp.

McLeod, Wilson. *Divided Gaels: Gaelic Cultural Identities in Scotland and Ireland c. 1200-1650*. Oxford: Oxford University Press, 2004.

Mid Argyll Kinship DNA Project, http://www.familytreedna.com/public/MidArgyllKinshipGroup/default.aspx.

Miller, Kerby A, ed. and others. *Irish Immigrants In The Land of Canaan*. Oxford: Oxford University Press, 2003.

Newton, Michael. *A Handbook of the Scottish Gaelic World*. Dublin: Four Courts Press, 2000.

Portlough Precinct Muster Rolls, 1630, http://ulsterheritage.com/store/files/MusterRollSurnames.pdf.

Ross, Anne. *The Folklore of the Scottish Highlands*. New York: Sterling Publishing, 1993.

Spencer, Elizabeth. *Writer's website*,
    http://www.elizabethspencerwriter.com.

Thomson, J Maitland, ed. *Inventory of Documents Relating to
    the Scrymgeour Family Estates 1611*. Edinburgh: J
    Skinner and Company, 1912.

Toner, Dr Peter M. *Confusing Identities: The Gaeltachtaí In
    New Brunswick, 1901*. The Seventeenth Biennial
    Ulster-American Heritage Symposium, 25-28 June
    2008. Centre for Migration Studies at the Ulster
    American Folk Park, Omagh, N Ireland.

White, Capt. Thomas P. *Archaeological Sketches in Scotland:
    Knapdale and Gigha*. London: Royal Collection, 1875.

Index

19548161R00135

Made in the USA
Middletown, DE
25 April 2015